Muller, Ulrike.
Persian cats :
everything about history
c2004.
33305209710593
gi   05/16/06

...ler and Colleen Power

...sian Cats

Everything About History, Purchase,
Care, Nutrition, Behavior, and Training

Full-color Photographs
Illustrations by Fritz W. Köhler

BARRON'S

²CONTENTS

THE PERSIAN PAST AND PRESENT

The traveler strolls through the Persian bazaar, searching out small treasures prized by Italian ladies. Spotting a remarkable cat, he draws nearer. A longhaired gray cat stretches out, enjoying the heat, though sporting fur draping 6 or more inches (15 cm) from the tail. Its eyes, huge, clear, coppery red jewels set in a very wide head, meet his gaze calmly, while huge soft paws reach out to grab his hand.

Origin of the Breed

The year was 1620, and the Italian, Pietro della Valle, had lived in and written extensively about Middle East countries. Now it was time for him and his new wife to return home, which meant finding presents for his patrons in Italy. Jewels, spices, silks—these traveled well, but court ladies yearned for more unique items. Quickly he struck a deal for four pairs of these remarkable gray longhairs, writing in his journals about the find. His is the first written record of the longhaired cats' introduction into Europe. These were the blue Persians that would, two centuries later, rule the show halls of the cat fancy. Enchanted, Pietro della Valle

A blue solid color Persian, first among all colors. Note the brilliant copper eyes and even coat color.

found what would become new toys for the merchants and court ladies of Europe.

The cats of Europe were sensible cats, short coated and fierce ratters. Sought out as witches' familiars, burned and drowned for centuries, the European cats were suspicious, shy biters. Longhaired cats born into the European countryside, where cats were tolerated as hard mousers, but not as protected pets, did not survive long. Their coats tangling and holding snow close to their skin, longhaired cats were impractical outdoor hunters. Only the shorthaired would thrive.

While the earliest mention of longhaired cats comes from the Middle East circa 1900 B.C., it was not until the 1600s that European travelers and traders began to bring the wonders of the longhair to Europe and that accurate records began to be kept. Throughout Asia and the Middle East, these early travelers discovered and tried to introduce similar longhaired cats; some were called Chinese cats, yet others named Indian cats, Afghanistan cats, and Russian cats. The Chinese cat sported not only long fur, but long floppy ears, similar to present-day lop-eared rabbits.

Persians vs. Angoras

In seventeenth century Turkey, in the ancient city of Ankara, a French naturalist, Nicholas Claude Fabri de Peiresc, found cats similar in ways to the gentle Persians of Pietro della Valle. Ankaran cats were highly prized pets of the Turks, sported longer coats, but not as thick as della Valle's gray cats. They were also more delicately boned. Fabri de Peiresc brought back several, in various colors, to the French court, calling them Angoras, after Ankara, their Turkish city of origin.

Through the seventeenth and eighteenth centuries, the other longhaired cats lost popularity, leaving the Persians and Angoras. The more exotic-looking Persians with their sturdier bones, wider heads, and thicker coats were crossed with the Angoras, fine-boned cats, with narrow heads, and fine long coats. By the early twentieth century, Angoras no longer existed outside of Turkey, where they would be rediscovered and reintroduced into the United States in the 1950s. Even today, the Angoras are confused in the public mind with the other longhaired cats, Persians.

The Importance of Pedigrees

The pedigree registries began with the British shows of the 1870s, where many colors of Persians were displayed, from the highly desired pale colors of blue, to the tabby coloration. The desire to breed to the best of the winners of these shows introduced the concept of formal registrations. The Governing Council of the Cat Fanciers became the first of these registries.

By the 1880s, cat clubs had crossed the Atlantic with shows held along the East Coast. Traveling by train and even by ship around the Straits of Magellan, the Persian fancy then became well established on the West Coast. American registries were well established by the 1900s, and began to insist on standards for breeding and judging. Today, the most important of these registries, registering more than 40,000 Persians a year, is the Cat Fanciers' Association, Inc., or CFA.

The First Cat Shows

Harrison Weir organized the first cat show ever known in London in 1971. The Longhairs, what we now in the United States call Persians, proved the most popular of all exhibits, with all but three of the show's entries designated as Longhairs. A Persian kitten was selected Best in Show. In his later years, Weir wrote the very first standards for cats, including the recognized Persian colors of that time: blues, whites, blacks, silvers, brown tabbies, and silver tabbies. These standards quickly grew to include reds, creams, and eventually blue-creams and tortoiseshells. Until the 1960s, the calico and bi-color were not accepted in the United States registries; Himalayans joined the Persian ranks in the 1970s.

Various cat associations in different countries have today written standards for both physical structure and more than 50 colors and patterns. In the United States, the CFA is the largest and most influential, with a very tight registry process, the equivalent of the AKC registry for dogs. Within CFA, Himalayans are recognized as Persians; Longhaired Exotics cannot be bred or shown as Persians, nor are new colors recognized for championship competition without a lengthy introduction process.

The Breed Standard

At exhibitions of pedigreed cats, judges award points for color and quality of fur, shape of head, eyes, build of body, tail, and general condition of the Persian cats. A perfect cat can score a maximum of 100 points.

Type: All Persian cats, no matter what color, should conform in type and body structure to the description in the standard.

Head: The round, massive head should sit on a short, thick neck. The small, round ears are set far apart and low on the head. Large, round eyes and a short, broad nose contribute to the "sweet expression" of the face. Typical for the profile of a Persian cat is the *stop*, or break, between the nose and the forehead. Full cheeks, broad and strong jaws, and a well-developed chin are also part of a typical Persian's head. An undershot jaw and other abnormalities of dentition are undesirable and should be avoided in breeding. Teary eyes, which are caused by a hereditary constriction of the tear ducts and nasal passages, are regarded as an abnormality.

The Official Show Standard of the Cat Fanciers' Association, Inc.

	Point Score
Head (Including size and shape of eyes, ear shape, and set)	30
Type (Including shape, size, bone, and length of tail)	20
Coat	10
Balance	5
Refinement	5
Color	20
Eye Color	10

Body build: A large or medium large, powerful body and short, sturdy legs should combine in an overall harmoniousness of shape. Persian cats are equally massive across the shoulders and rump, with well-developed muscles and a horizontal back. The large, round paws have five digits on the front feet and four on the back feet. The toes are closely spaced, with long tufts of fur between them.

Tail: The tail is short, in good proportion to body length, without bends or kinks, and covered with thick, feathery fur.

Coat: The fur of a Persian cat is dense and full, of silky and soft consistency, standing out from the body, and full of sheen and movement. Except on the face, it is of an even length all over and forms an exceptionally impressive, thick ruff around the neck.

The most frequently seen cat in the mass media, the Persian is the epitome of luxury, and the most immediately identified by the general public as purebred. A gray Persian is called blue, an orange Persian is listed as a red, and a light tan is called a cream. Fortunately, a white is a white, and a black is a black.

Color Varieties

At cat shows you can see Persian cats in many color varieties that are the result of long years of planned breeding. Many of these colors are never or only rarely seen in ordinary outdoor cats because they either are inherited through recessive genes, or—like the color white—they represent a disadvantage for an animal living unprotected in nature.

Solid: Whites are often born with black head markings that fade gradually over several months. Creams may develop dark points and become Himalayan. Tabby bars may fade to become shaded coats. Blacks often have ghostly tabby bars, visible when the light hits the coat just right.

Smoke: A smoke kitten is born a solid color—black, red, cream, or blue, often with

Like calicos, the blue-cream is usually female. The male is usually sterile.

lighter face markings. By three weeks the fur may begin to develop the gorgeous sharp white undercoat. This undercoat will often fade, only to reappear in adulthood. Or it may simply be a solid color kitten that spiked a fever, causing a lighter line of color to mark the growing coat.

Tabby: Tabby kittens are often born with just a few markings at the eyebrows and a lighter chin, but by three weeks, as the coat grows longer, the strong tabby bars begin to appear. Bold round circles on the side mean a classic tabby; narrow stripes mean a mackerel tabby.

Himalayan: Most amazing may be the Himalayans. Not only are they born creamy white and begin to develop their color points at three weeks of age, but the color points develop on the cooler parts of the cat—the tail, the paws, the ears. Should the Himalayan develop a penchant for the floor furnace, it may also display the pattern of your furnace grate on its sides!

How Many Persian Colors Are There?

Various cat associations in different countries have today written standards for more than 50 colors of Persians. Included here are the most popular colors. These colors are often combined with patterns, specifically white, tipped, and Himalayan.

Newest colors are the lilac and chocolate colors, inheriting these rare genes from their Himalayan background.

Solid- or Self-colored Persians: White, black, blue, chocolate, lilac, red, and cream. Black and red commonly occur in ordinary cats, too, but the other colors are rare in household cats that mate freely. White is an especially important color in Persian cats. This is not albino white, which is very rare in cats, but the white carried by a dominant gene. That means that a white cat can, depending on its heredity, have genes for any other color.

Multicolored Persians: Red-and-black Persian cats are called tortoiseshell. If the red and the black are "diluted," the result is blue-cream. Tortoiseshell and blue-cream Persian cats, even if they have some white, are nearly always female animals.

Bi-Colors and Calicos: White patched cats are very popular today. The more white the better for show. Calico, tortoiseshell, and blue-cream males are extremely unusual. Because two X chromosomes are female, a male with 2X is generally sterile. The combination of blue-cream and white is also called dilute calico.

Colorpoint: This name is given to Himalayan cats with Siamese markings. This strain was developed many years ago by crossing Siamese with Persian cats. The result of the crossing was a cat with the build and the long fur of a Persian but with the coloring and markings of a Siamese. These beautiful cats are regarded as Persians by the Cat Fanciers' Association.

Tabby Persians: These are some of the oldest Persian breeds. The tabby pattern occurs in many different colors and is characterized by so-called *ticking*. Ticking means that the individual hairs have two to three bands of light and dark color, with the tips always dark. In longhaired Persians the tabby pattern is not as obvious as in shorthaired breeds, which have smooth fur that lies down flat.

"Tipped" Persians: Cats with coats where the color is restricted to the tips of the hairs. The tipping can vary in degree. If, in a black Persian, only about $\frac{1}{8}$th of the hair is tipped dark, we have what is called a chinchilla Persian. Depending on the extent and the color of the tipping, there are a number of distinct color varieties. Instead of black, the tipping can be blue. Cream- or red-tipped Persians are called cameos. If the tipping is very strong, that is, if almost the entire hair is colored, the white undercoat practically disappears. These cats are called smoke Persians; they, too, come in all kinds of colors.

Persian Colors in North America

The would-be owner of a Persian kitten may find it bewildering to be faced with 50 Persian colors recognized by the Cat Fanciers' Association. But do not be daunted. All Persians are decorative; all make delightful pets.

White: Pure glistening white. *Nose leather and paw pads:* Pink. *Eye color:* Deep blue or brilliant copper. Odd-eyed whites shall have one blue and one copper eye with equal color depth.

	Color of the Tipping	
Length of the Tipping	Red or Cream	Black
1/8 of hair	Shell Cameo	Chinchilla
1/3 (1/8–1/2) of hair	Shaded Cameo	Shaded Silver
More than 1/2 to 2/3 of hair	Red or Cream Smoke	Smoke

Black: Dense coal black, sound from roots to tip of fur. Free from any tinge of rust on tips or smoke undercoat. *Nose leather:* Black. *Paw pads:* Black or brown. *Eye color:* Brilliant copper.

Blue: Blue, lighter shade preferred, one level tone from nose to tip of tail. Sound to the roots. A sound darker shade is more acceptable than an unsound lighter shade. *Nose leather and paw pads:* Blue. *Eye color:* Brilliant copper.

Red: Deep, rich, clear, brilliant red; without shading, markings, or ticking. Lips and chin the same color as coat. *Nose leather and paw pads:* Brick red. *Eye color:* Brilliant copper.

Cream: One level shade of buff cream, without markings. Sound to the roots. Lighter shades preferred. *Nose leather and paw pads:* Pink. *Eye color:* Brilliant copper.

Chinchilla: Undercoat pure white. Coat on back, flanks, head, and tail sufficiently tipped with black to give the characteristic sparkling silver appearance. Legs may be slightly shaded with tipping. Chin and ear tufts, stomach and chest, pure white. Rims of eyes, lips, and nose outlined with black. *Nose leather:* Brick red. *Paw pads:* Black. *Eye color:* Green or blue-green. Disqualify for incorrect eye color (copper, yellow, gold, amber, or any color other than green or blue-green).

Shaded Silver: Undercoat white with a mantle of black tipping shading down from side, face, and tail from dark on the ridge to white on the chin, chest, stomach, and under the tail. Legs to be the same tone as the face. The general effect to be much darker than a chinchilla. Rims of eyes, lips, and nose outlined with black. *Nose leather:* Brick red. *Paw pads:* Black. *Eye color:* Green or blue-green. Disqualify for incorrect eye color (copper, yellow, gold, amber, or any color other than green or blue-green).

Chinchilla Golden: Undercoat rich warm cream. Coat on back, flanks, head, and tail sufficiently tipped with seal brown to give golden appearance. Legs may be slightly shaded with tipping. Chin and ear tufts, stomach, and chest, cream. Rims of eyes, lips, and nose outlined with seal brown. *Nose leather:* Deep rose. *Paw pads:* Seal brown. *Eye color:* Green or blue-green. Disqualify for incorrect eye color (copper, yellow, gold, amber, or any color other than green or blue-green).

Smoke Tortoiseshell: White undercoat deeply tipped with black and clearly defined, unbrindled patches of red- and cream-tipped hairs as in the pattern of the tortoiseshell. Cat in repose appears tortoiseshell. In motion the white undercoat is clearly apparent. Face and ears tortoiseshell pattern with narrow band of white at the base of the hairs next to the skin, which may be seen only when fur is parted. White ruff and ear tufts. Blaze of red or cream tipping on face is desirable. *Eye color:* Brilliant copper.

A very rare golden chinchilla (left) show kitten. The shaded silver (right) littermate, while lovely, has a much narrower head and will likely go to a pet home. Goldens are recessive colors and can appear in silver litters. A silver kitten cannot appear in a litter of goldens.

Odd-eyed white. The black head cap, often covering the entire forehead at birth, has now faded to a small gray area near the left ear, disappearing completely in adulthood. Deafness is a concern in all white cats, regardless of eye color, with an onset around the age of two months.

This exquisite solid red male would make a wonderful cross with a blue-cream female.

A Persian relative. If the Persian coat is too hard to work with, consider a shorthaired version—the Exotic Shorthair!

Blue-cream Smoke: White undercoat deeply tipped with blue, with clearly defined patches of cream as in the pattern of the blue-cream. Cat in repose appears blue-cream. In motion the white undercoat is clearly apparent. Face and ears blue-cream pattern with narrow band of white at the base of the hair next to the skin that may be seen only when fur is parted. White ruff and ear tufts. Blaze of cream tipping on face is desirable. *Eye color:* Brilliant copper.

Classic Tabby Pattern: Markings dense, clearly defined, and broad. Legs evenly barred with bracelets coming up to meet the body markings. Tail evenly ringed. Several unbroken necklaces on neck and upper chest, the more the better. Frown marks on forehead form intricate letter M. Unbroken line runs back from outer corner of eye. Swirls on cheeks. Vertical lines over back of head extend to shoulder markings, which are in the shape of a butterfly with both upper and lower wings distinctly outlined and marked with dots inside outline. Back markings consist of a vertical line down the spine from butterfly to tail with a vertical stripe paralleling it on each side, the three stripes well separated by stripes of the ground color. Large solid blotch on each side to be encircled by one or more unbroken rings. Side markings should be the same on both sides. Double vertical row of buttons on chest and stomach.

Mackerel Tabby Pattern: Markings dense, clearly defined, and all narrow pencilings. Legs evenly barred with narrow bracelets coming up to meet the body markings. Tails barred. Necklaces on neck and chest distinct, like so many chains. Head barred with an M on the forehead. Unbroken lines running back from the eyes. Lines running down the head to meet the shoulders. Spine lines run together to form a narrow saddle. Narrow pencilings run around body.

Patched Tabby Pattern: A Patched Tabby (Torbie) is an established silver, brown, or blue tabby with patches or red and/or cream.

Brown Patched Tabby: Ground color brilliant coppery brown with classic or mackerel tabby markings of dense black with patches of red and/or cream clearly defined on both body and extremities; a blaze of red and/or cream on the face is desirable. Lips and chin the same shade as the rings around the eyes. *Eye color:* Brilliant copper.

Blue Patched Tabby: Ground color, including lips and chin, pale bluish ivory with classic or mackerel tabby markings of very deep blue affording a good contrast with ground color. Patches of cream clearly defined on both body and extremities; a blaze of cream on the face is desirable. Warm fawn overtones or patina over the whole. *Eye color:* Brilliant copper.

Silver Patched Tabby: Ground color, including lips and chin, pale silver with classic or mackerel tabby markings of dense black with patches of red and/or cream clearly defined on both body and extremities. A blaze of red and/or cream on the face is desirable. *Eye color:* Brilliant copper or hazel.

Silver Tabby: Ground color, including lips and chin, pale, clear silver. Markings dense black. *Nose leather:* Brick red. *Paw pads:* Black. *Eye color:* Green, hazel, or brilliant copper.

Red Tabby: Ground color red. Markings deep, rich red. Lips and chin red. *Nose leather and paw pads:* Brick red. *Eye color:* Brilliant copper.

Brown Tabby: Ground color brilliant coppery brown. Markings dense black. Lips and chin the same shade as the rings around the eyes. Back of leg black from paw to heel. *Nose leather:*

Brick red. *Paw pads:* Black or brown. *Eye color:* Brilliant copper.

Blue Tabby: Ground color, including lips and chin, pale bluish ivory. Markings a very deep blue affording a good contrast with ground color. Warm fawn overtones or patina over the whole. *Nose leather:* Old rose. *Paw pads:* Rose. *Eye color:* Brilliant copper.

Cream Tabby: Ground color, including lips and chin, very pale cream. Markings of buff or cream sufficiently darker than the ground color to afford good contrast but remaining within the dilute color range. *Nose leather and paw pads:* Pink. *Eye color:* Brilliant copper.

Cameo Tabby: Ground color off-white. Markings red. *Nose leather and paw pads:* Rose. *Eye color:* Brilliant copper.

Shaded Golden: Undercoat rich warm cream with a mantle of seal brown tipping shading down from sides, face, and tail from dark on the ridge to cream on the chin, chest, stomach, and under the tail. Legs to be the same tone as the face. The general effect to be much darker than a chinchilla. Rims of eyes, lips, and nose outlined with seal brown. *Nose leather:* Deep rose. *Paw pads:* Seal brown. *Eye color:* Green or blue-green. Disqualify for incorrect eye color (copper, yellow, gold, amber, or any color other than green or blue-green).

Shell Cameo (Red Chinchilla): Undercoat white, the coat on the back, flanks, head, and tail to be sufficiently tipped with red to give the characteristic sparkling appearance. Face and legs may be very slightly shaded with tipping. Chin, ear tufts, stomach, and chest white. *Nose leather and paw pads:* Rose. *Eye color:* Brilliant copper.

Shaded Cameo (Red Shaded): Undercoat white with a mantle of red tipping shading down the sides, face, and tail from dark on the ridge to white on the chin, chest, stomach, and under the tail. Legs to be the same tone as face. The general effect to be much redder than the shell cameo. *Nose leather, rims of eyes, and paw pads:* Rose. *Eye color:* Brilliant copper.

Shell Tortoiseshell: Undercoat white. Coat on the back, flanks, head, and tail to be delicately tipped in black with well-defined patches of red and cream tipped hairs as in the pattern of the tortoiseshell. Face and legs may be slightly shaded with tipping. Chin, ear tufts, stomach, and chest white to very slightly tipped. Blaze of red or cream tipping on face is desirable. *Eye color:* Brilliant copper.

Shaded Tortoiseshell: Undercoat white. Mantle of black tipping and clearly defined patches of red and cream tipped hairs as in the pattern of the tortoiseshell. Shading down the sides, face, and tail from dark on the ridge to slightly tipped or white on the chin, chest, stomach, legs, and under the tail. The general effect is to be much darker than the shell tortoiseshell. Blaze of red or cream tipping on the face is desirable. *Eye color:* Brilliant copper.

Black Smoke: White undercoat, deeply tipped with black. Cat in repose appears black. In motion the white undercoat is clearly apparent. Points and mask black with narrow band of white at base of hairs next to skin which may be seen only when fur is parted. Light silver frill and ear tufts. *Nose leather and paw pads:* Black. *Eye color:* Brilliant copper.

Blue Smoke: White undercoat, deeply tipped with blue. Cat in repose appears blue. In motion the white undercoat is clearly apparent. Points and mask blue with narrow band of white at base of hairs next to skin which may be seen only when fur is parted. White frill and ear

A blue-cream female with extraordinary boning.

An exquisite solid color cream with brilliant copper eyes, a mature broad head, and wonderful small ears.

A blue point Himalayan kitten with excellent required blue eye color. The color points darken with age and with injuries.

A dilute calico or blue-cream with white. Genetically, most calicos are female with xx chromosomes, while the very few calico males are usually xxy, rendering them sterile.

A classic brown tabby with glossy, gleaming, healthy coat.

This shaded silver has an excellent rounded forehead called "doming" that accentuates the beautiful, small, widely separated ears.

tufts. *Nose leather and paw pads:* Blue. *Eye color:* Brilliant copper.

Cameo Smoke (Red Smoke): White undercoat, deeply tipped with red. Cat in repose appears red. In motion the white undercoat is clearly apparent. Points and mask red with narrow band of white at base of hairs next to skin that may be seen only when fur is parted. White frill and ear tufts. *Nose leather, rims of eyes, and paw pads:* Rose. *Eye color:* Brilliant copper.

Calico: White with unbrindled patches of black and red. White predominant on underparts. *Eye color:* Brilliant copper or odd-eyed.

Dilute Calico: White with unbrindled patches of blue and cream. White predominant on underparts. *Eye color:* Brilliant copper or odd-eyed.

Bi-color: Black and white, blue and white, red and white, cream and white, chocolate and white, and lilac and white. White feet, legs undersides, chest, and muzzle. Inverted V blaze on face desirable. White under tail and white collar allowable. *Eye color:* Brilliant copper or odd-eyed.

Persian Van Bi-color: Black and white, red and white, blue and white, or cream and white. White cat with color confined to the extremities; head, tail, and legs. One or two small colored patches on body allowable. *Eye color:* Brilliant copper or odd-eyed.

Peke-Faced Red and **Peke-Faced Red Tabby:** The Peke-Faced cat should conform in color, markings, and general type to the standards set forth for the red and red tabby Persian cat. The head should resemble as much as possible that of the Pekingese dog from which it gets its name. Nose should be very short and depressed, or indented between the eyes. There

should be a decidedly wrinkled muzzle. Eyes round, large, and full, set wide apart, prominent and brilliant. Very few Peke-Faced lines exist, and they are seldom seen today. There is a distinct ridge across the brow of the Peke-Faced cats; and while it may recur in other colors than red, only red and red tabby Peke-Faced cats may be shown.

Parti-color Division Colors

Tortoiseshell: Black with patches of red or softly intermingled areas of red on both body and extremities. Presence of several shades of red acceptable. *Nose leather and paw pads:* Black and/or brick red. *Eye color:* Brilliant copper.

Blue-cream: Blue with patches of cream or softly intermingled areas of cream on both body and extremities. Lighter shades preferred. *Nose leather and paw pads:* Blue and/or pink. *Eye color:* Brilliant copper.

Chocolate Tortoiseshell: Rich, warm chocolate brown with patches of red or softly intermingled areas of red on both body and extremities. Presence of several shades of red acceptable. *Nose leather:* Brown, brick red, and/or pink. *Paw pads:* Brick red, cinnamon pink, and/or pink. *Eye color:* Brilliant copper.

Lilac-cream: Rich, warm pinkish toned lavender with patches of cream or softly intermingled areas of cream on both body and extremities. *Nose leather:* Lavender, lavender pink, and/or pink. *Paw pads:* Lavender pink and/or pink. *Eye color:* Brilliant copper.

New Colors

Each year more colors of Persians are recognized for championship. Most recently, all ranges of colors in the chocolate and lilac series have been added, from solid chocolates and lilacs to smoke chocolate/lilacs to bi-color chocolates/lilacs, with even chocolate tabbies earning Grand championship status.

Please note that, as with other Persian colors, these colors have distinctive paw pad colors, and that judges will be checking to make sure there is correct paw and nose leather color. Of course, as with other colors of patched tabbies, bi-colors, and parti-color cats, the paw pads are allowed to be spotted with color.

Chocolate: Rich, warm chocolate-brown, sound from roots to tip of fur. *Nose leather:* Brown. *Paw pads:* Cinnamon-pink. *Eye color:* Brilliant copper.

Lilac: Rich, warm lavender with a pinkish tone, sound and even throughout. *Nose leather:* Lavender. *Paw pads:* Pink. *Eye color:* Brilliant copper.

Chocolate Tabby (classic, mackerel): Ground color milk chocolate. Tabby markings a deep, dark chocolate affording sufficient contrast with ground color. Lips and chin the same shade as rings around the eyes. *Nose leather:* Brown and/or brick red. *Paw pads:* Brick red to cinnamon-pink. *Eye color:* Brilliant copper.

Chocolate Patched Tabby (classic, mackerel): Ground color milk chocolate. Tabby markings a deep, dark chocolate affording sufficient contrast to ground color with patches or softly intermingled areas of red. Lips and chin the same color as rings around the eyes. *Nose leather:* Brown, brick red, and/or cinnamon pink. *Paw pads:* Brick red, cinnamon pink, and/or coral. *Eye color:* Brilliant copper.

Lilac Tabby (classic, mackerel): Ground color pale frosty lavender with a pinkish patina. Tabby markings a darker lavender affording sufficient contrast with ground color.

Lips and chin the same color as rings around the eyes. *Nose leather:* Lavender. *Paw pads:* Pink. *Eye color:* Brilliant copper.

Lilac Patched Tabby (classic, mackerel): Ground color pale frosty lavender with a pinkish patina. Tabby markings a darker lavender affording sufficient contrast to ground color with patches or softly intermingled areas of cream. Lips and chin the same color as rings around the eyes. *Nose leather:* Lavender and/or pink. *Paw pads:* Lavender pink and/or pink. *Eye color:* Brilliant copper.

Chocolate Calico: A tri-color cat of chocolate, red, and white. The red and the chocolate should appear as clear, unbridled patches. As a preferred minimum, the cat should have white feet, legs, undersides, chest, and muzzle. Less white than this minimum should be penalized proportionately.

Lilac Calico: A tri-color cat of lilac, cream, and white. The lilac and the cream should appear as clear, unbridled patches. As a preferred minimum, the cat should have white feet, legs, undersides, chest, and muzzle. Less white than this minimum should be penalized proportionately.

With the addition of odd-eyes to the Bi-color Division, the following are the allowed eye colors in bi-colors:

Eye Color: Brilliant copper, blue or odd-eyed, with noted exception. Odd-eyed bi-colors should have one blue and one copper eye with equal color depth. *Exception:* Silver tabby and white, silver patched tabby and white, blue silver tabby and white, and blue silver patched tabby and white may also have green or hazel eye color. These colors in odd-eyed cats should have one blue and one green, hazel, or brilliant copper eye with equal color depth.

A young blue-cream female with highly desirable, widely separated eyes that are still khaki colored. The eyes will clear to fiery brilliant copper by eight months of age.

A chinchilla silver Persian. Some small amount of tearing and an eye squint on such an immaculately groomed cat is a warning to check the eyes closely for any signs of injury.

Brown tabby kittens. Notice that one has excellent stripes on the neck and ruff. These are called "necklaces," and are especially sought after by judges.

A blue and white bi-color kitten. With too many body spots to be classified as a "Van," this kitten is perfect in every way. Anything sparkly attracts cats of all ages.

The smokes and other tipped colors have also added many new possibilities:

Chocolate Calico Smoke: A tri-color cat of chocolate, red, and white. The chocolate and the red should appear as clear, unbridled patches with a white undercoat. As a preferred minimum, the cat should have white feet, legs, undersides, chest, and muzzle. Less white than this minimum should be penalized proportionately.

Lilac Calico Smoke: A tri-color cat of lilac, cream, and white. The lilac and the cream should appear as clear, unbridled patches with a white undercoat. As a preferred minimum, the cat should have white feet, legs, undersides, chest, and muzzle. Less white than this minimum should be penalized proportionately.

Shell Cameo and White, Shell Cream and White, Shell Calico, Shell Dilute Calico, Shell Chocolate Calico, Shell Lilac Calico: A bi-colored or tri-colored cat of white and colored portions, the colored portions of the cat to conform to the currently established shell color description. As a preferred minimum, the cat should have white feet, legs, undersides, chest, and muzzle. Less white than this minimum should be penalized proportionately.

Shaded Cameo and White, Shaded Cream and White, Shaded Calico, Shaded Dilute Calico, Shaded Chocolate Calico, Shaded Lilac Calico: A bi-colored or tri-colored cat of white and colored portions, the colored portions of the cat to conform to the currently established shaded color description. As a preferred minimum, the cat should have white feet, legs, undersides, chest, and muzzle. Less white than this minimum should be penalized proportionately.

Within the Himalayan division, these colors are now recognized:

Himalayan (Point) Pattern: *Body:* Clear color is preferred with subtle shading allowed. Allowance should be made for darker color in older cats, but there must be a definite contrast between body color and point color. The points, consisting of ears, legs, feet, tail, and mask show the basic color of the cat. The ideal mask extends from above the eyes, down through the chin, and stretches beyond the eyes from side to side.

Chocolate Point: *Body:* Ivory. *Points:* Milk-chocolate color, warm in tone. *Nose leather and paw pads:* Cinnamon pink. *Eye color:* Deep vivid blue.

Seal Point: *Body:* Even pale fawn to cream, warm in tone, shading gradually into lighter color on the stomach and chest. *Points:* Deep seal brown. *Nose leather and paw pads:* Seal brown. *Eye color:* Deep vivid blue.

Lilac Point: *Body:* Glacial white. *Points:* Frosty gray with pinkish tone. *Nose leather and paw pads:* Lavender pink. *Eye color:* Deep vivid blue.

Blue Point: *Body:* Bluish white, cold in tone, shading gradually to white on stomach and chest. *Points:* Blue. *Nose leather and paw pads:* Slate blue. *Eye color:* Deep vivid blue.

Flame (Red) Point: *Body:* Creamy white. *Points:* Deep orange flame to deep red. *Nose leather and paw pads:* Flesh to coral pink. *Eye color:* Deep vivid blue.

Cream Point: *Body:* Creamy white. *Points:* Buff cream. *Nose leather and paw pads:* Flesh to coral pink. *Eye color:* Deep vivid blue.

Tortie Point: *Body:* Creamy white or pale fawn. *Points:* Seal with unbridled patches of red and/or cream. *Nose leather and paw pads:* Seal brown and/or coral pink. *Eye color:* Deep vivid blue.

Blue-cream Point: Body: Bluish white or creamy white, shading gradually to white on the stomach and chest. *Points:* Blue with patches of cream. *Nose leather and paw pads:* Slate blue and/or pink. *Eye color:* Deep vivid blue.

Chocolate-Tortie Point: *Body:* Ivory. *Points:* Chocolate with unbridled patches of red and/or cream. *Nose leather and paw pads:* Cinnamon pink and/or coral pink. *Eye color:* Deep vivid blue.

Lilac-Cream Point: *Body:* Glacial white. *Points:* Lilac with patches of cream. *Nose leather and paw pads:* Lavender pink and/or pink. *Eye color:* Deep vivid blue.

Himalayan Lynx (Point) Pattern: Mask must be clearly lined with dark stripes, must be vertical, and must form the classic "M" on the forehead; horizontal on the cheeks. The mask contains light rings around the eyes and dark spots on light whisker pads, clearly outlined in dark color edges. Inner ear light with ticking on outer ear. Markings dense, clearly defined and broad. Legs evenly barred with bracelets. Tail barred with lighter underside. No striping or mottling on body.

Seal Lynx Point: *Body:* Pale cream to fawn, warm in tone. *Points:* Beige-brown ticked with darker brown tabby markings. *Nose leather:* Seal brown or brick red. *Paw pads:* Seal brown. *Eye color:* Deep vivid blue.

Blue Lynx Point: *Body:* Bluish white, cold in tone. *Points:* Light, silvery blue, ticked with darker blue tabby markings. *Nose leather:* Blue or old rose. *Paw pads:* Blue. *Eye color:* Deep vivid blue.

Flame (Red) Lynx Point: *Body:* Creamy white. *Points:* Deep orange flame ticked with deep red tabby markings. *Nose leather and paw pads:* Flesh to coral pink. *Eye color:* Deep vivid blue.

Cream Lynx Point: *Body:* Creamy white, significantly lighter in tone than the points. *Points:* Pale cream ticked with dark cream tabby markings. *Nose leather and paw pads:* Flesh to coral pink. *Eye color:* Deep vivid blue.

Tortie Lynx Point: *Body:* Creamy white or pale fawn. *Points:* Beige-brown with dark brown tabby markings and patches of red. *Nose leather and paw pads:* Seal brown, brick red, and/or coral pink. *Eye color:* Deep vivid blue.

Blue-Cream Lynx Point: *Body:* Bluish white, cold in tone. *Points:* Blue with darker blue tabby markings and patches of cream. *Nose leather and paw pads:* Blue, old rose, and/or pink. *Eye color:* Deep vivid blue.

Chocolate Lynx Point: *Body:* Ivory. *Points:* Milk-chocolate ticked with darker chocolate tabby markings. *Nose leather and paw pads:* Cinnamon pink or coral pink. *Eye color:* Deep vivid blue.

Lilac Lynx Point: *Body:* Glacial white. *Points:* Pale frosty gray with pinkish tone ticked with darker lilac tabby markings. *Nose leather and paw pads:* Lavender pink. *Eye color:* Deep vivid blue.

Chocolate-Tortie Lynx Point: *Body:* Ivory. *Points:* Milk-chocolate ticked with darker chocolate tabby markings and patches of red. *Nose leather and paw pads:* Cinnamon pink and/or coral pink. *Eye color:* Deep vivid blue.

Lilac-Cream Lynx Point: *Body:* Glacial white. *Points:* Pale frosty grey with pinkish tone ticked with darker lilac tabby markings and patches of cream. *Nose leather and paw pads:* Lavender pink and/or coral pink. *Eye color:* Deep vivid blue.

CONSIDERATIONS BEFORE YOU BUY

Do you enjoy a cat that follows you from room to room? Lying upside down in your arms, wrapping its paws around your hand, begging for a chin scratch? Do you have an apartment with neighbors who might complain about a noisy cat? Do you love combing your daughter's hair, patiently untangling mats that form seemingly overnight? Then the Persian may be ideal for you.

Your Lifestyle and a Persian Cat

Anyone intending to share a home with as highly developed and demanding a pet as a Persian cat has to be well informed about the needs of cats and has to give careful thought to a number of factors to prevent future unpleasant surprises:

✔ If you get a cat, you will be responsible for an animal whose life and well-being will depend entirely on your care. You should be fully aware of this.

✔ You should be willing and able to devote much of your leisure time to your pet. This is true for the entire, long life of the cat, which may be as long as 25 years.

Whites may be copper-eyed, blue-eyed, or odd-eyed. This blue-eyed beauty is a very rare specimen.

✔ Because of its long, fine fur, a Persian cat needs intensive grooming in addition to the normal time spent daily with the cat.

✔ Will you retain your equanimity if something is broken now and then, especially while the animal is young and full of energy?

✔ Remember that cats often use furniture for sharpening their claws.

✔ Don't forget that owning a cat costs money on an ongoing basis for food, litter, grooming, and preventive health care.

If You Like to Travel

If you like to take lengthy vacations, you should, before getting a cat, consider who will look after it while you are away from home or where you can board it. It is always best if the cat can stay in its familiar home and be looked after by a cat-loving and reliable person it already knows. If this is not feasible, perhaps you can take your cat to a relative or friend's house. Places that board cats can be found just about anywhere, too, but it is best to inspect and perhaps compare several before leaving your cat there. If you spend your entire vacation in a rented cottage or in some similar arrangement, your cat might enjoy being taken along. (For more on traveling, see page 60.)

Legal Questions and Human Relationships

Rented quarters: If you rent, ask the landlord for written permission to keep a cat in your apartment.

Insurance: Generally, a private liability policy will pay for damage your cat has done to other people or their property. There are also health insurance policies for pets that usually cover costs for surgery, diagnostic services, and medicine.

TIP

What to Do When a Baby Arrives

Quite often a couple with a cat expect their first child. Sometimes this causes the young parents worry and exaggerated fears, especially if they have been given alarmist advice. Apart from certain precautionary measures to be taken during pregnancy against the slight chance of toxoplasmosis infection, the presence of a cat in the household with a baby calls for no special arrangements beyond the usual standards of hygiene.

Other members of the family and of the household: Of course, the whole family and anyone else living in the household should be consulted and agree to the acquisition of a cat, as not everyone likes sharing their bed pillow with a cat, no matter how sweetly it may purr. Life with a cat is more trying than usual when an unspayed female is in heat and cries a lot, and living in cramped quarters with an unaltered tomcat can be nearly unbearable.

Neighbors: It is a good idea to find out how your immediate neighbors feel about cats and to tell them about the advantages of having a cat around. Many cats that live in the country or in the suburbs occasionally visit a neighbor's garden and may bury their excrement in a vegetable bed there. This can give rise to serious altercations with the owner of the garden. Most homes are in city residential areas, which forbid the keeping of animals for breeding or resale. Neighbors can report you to the County Zoning Department for such violations.

Persian Cats and Other Pets

✔ *Dogs* and cats usually coexist peacefully if they both joined the household when young. An intelligent dog that loves its master unconditionally soon learns to accept a new cat as a family member. It is a little more difficult to get a cat that is already established and a new dog used to each other, but usually a *modus vivendi* without friction can be achieved here, too. The communications difficulties between cats and dogs—difficulties that arise from their different innate methods of signaling dominance and submission—are usually overcome by these intelligent animals in time and to the degree necessary in the given situation.

✔ *Mice*, hamsters, gerbils, guinea pigs, and dwarf rabbits instantly trigger a cat's hunting instinct. Their size and behavior may designate them as prey animals in the eyes of the cat.

✔ *Birds* hopping around busily in their cage fascinate Persian cats and may quickly fall victim to a cat if it can catch them.

✔ *Fish* are most attractive to cats; they are among a cat's favorite culinary delicacies. An aquarium should, therefore, always be safely covered, so that the cat is not tempted to fish for its supper.

Important: A harmonious coexistence that harbors no dangers for the smaller pet is possible only in rare cases. A cat has to have learned as a kitten to accept the other pet, and its hunting instinct should remain subdued even later on. Similarly, dogs should not be left alone with cats, because this may arouse canine hunting instincts.

Children and Cats

Cats are highly developed and in many respects demanding animals. Keeping them when there are small children in the house can therefore be recommended only with reservations. Cats love to spend much of their day sleeping peacefully. Most loathe being pursued constantly and held against their will.

All this should be considered before a family with children decides to get a cat. If the parents have experience with cats and know the animals' needs, they can guide the children and prevent mistreatment that might, in extreme cases, lead to abnormal behavior in the cat. A child who has genuine, consistent interest in

the cat and approaches it with understanding can gradually take over the responsibility of feeding and caring for the animal.

Financial Considerations

The price of a cat is seldom equal to the expected upkeep. Even a kitten from the animal shelter will cost $35 to adopt, plus the expense of the veterinary visit for shots could cost another $100, so even for a stray kitten, you are starting out spending close to $150. This makes a pedigreed kitten, with its first three shots already completed, a comparative bargain at $250 to $800 for a pet, $1,000 to $5,000 for a show-potential investment. Sometimes there are opportunities to get an adult animal through on-line Persian rescue groups or from a retiring show exhibitor.

Food: You should figure on $1 to $1.50 a day for food. This includes vitamins and occasional treats.

Accessories: Depending on your own ideas and tastes, you can buy everything a Persian cat needs for very little money or spend a couple of hundred dollars on designer cat trees.

Veterinary care: Your cat will have to be wormed regularly and vaccinated annually, if it gets sick, there will be additional costs for treatment and medications. Also keep in mind that neutering a cat costs money.

Boarding or pet-sitting: If you take vacations, you will need to arrange for your Persian to be boarded or hire a pet sitter. Persians' thick long coats require expert and gentle hands. Expect to pay $10 dollars a day for this service.

The kitten in the pet shop window will hardly resemble the magnificent show kitties, and more importantly, you will have no notion of the parentage, either by behavior or by the type of home environment that nurtured the basic personality.

Breeders

It is best to buy a Persian cat from a reputable breeder; be sure to take the time to investigate how the animal is housed and what it is fed. Knowledgeable breeders will help you with advice and answer questions you may have later on. Associations maintain lists of breeders in every part of the country, and occasionally, Persians are advertised for sale in the newspaper. Going to shows of pedigreed cats is also a good way to find a kitten. Some cities have outlawed the keeping of breeding cats so you may find the breeders reluctant to invite you into their homes; this makes the show hall often the only method of access to the purchase of a pedigreed kitten. Keep in mind that most associations will not allow kittens under the age of four months into a show hall as they are not fully vaccinated.

This lovely dilute calico will likely go to a pet home, because she lacks the copious amounts of white that judges and breeders are looking for in the ring.

It is important to note that with all the millions of cats born in this country each year, only 40,000 or so are purebred Persians, so contacting reputable breeders is the best way to get yourself on the waiting list for these healthy kittens. Most pet shops have given up selling pedigreed kittens, as many of the kitten mills that supply the dealers have difficulty passing the strict requirements of the Cat Fanciers' Association, which automatically inspects any cattery registering excess litters each year.

You will want to find a cat show to locate reputable breeders, though a search of the local newspaper, or a call to CFA Central Office in New Jersey (see Information, page 92) may put you on the track to finding the right kitten. CFA maintains a registry of breeders in each area of the country.

Once you find your breeder you will often be asked questions about your background as a pet owner, your home situation, whether you are an apartment dweller, have children, other

TIP

Questions the Breeder Is Likely to Ask
✔ Why do you want a Persian?
✔ What is your experience with longhaired cats?
✔ Do you have other cats and dogs? What kinds and ages?
✔ Do you have children? What ages?
✔ Have you introduced a young kitten into your home before?
✔ May we call your veterinarian for references?
✔ Do you think you might want to show or breed?
✔ Do you want a male or female?

Sexing kittens. On the left is a little tomcat; on the right, a female kitten. The space between the penis and the anus is larger than that between the vagina and the anus. The sexual orifice of a male kitten is round, that of a female, slit-like.

pets, and so on, so be prepared. These are special kittens, with very special breeders. Many even have their own written contracts and guarantees. They often maintain lists of people desiring kittens, so you may need to call them back several times over a period of months.

Show Cat or Fancier's Pet?

Recognizing the subtle differences between two littermates, a show kitten priced up to $10,000 and a pet kitten being offered for $550, may be difficult. A pet black kitten may have the same short nose, but a disqualifying color fault, such as a small patch of white (locket) on the chest or belly, or a pet silver kitten may not have complete eye "mascara" markings.

A Show Cat

Persian kittens advertised as being "of show quality" or "suitable for breeding" are the most expensive. A breeder has to wait a long time before a kitten is born that will grow into a cat that matches the breed standard (see page 7) perfectly and is as flawless as possible.

A Fancier's Pet

Any breeder will have litters with kittens that don't live up to the standard in shape or in color. If they are healthy, affectionate, and what is commonly regarded as beautiful, a breeder will often sell them cheaper to a fancier because they can't be used for pedigreed breeding. Even if you have no interest in breeding cats, you should still choose a purebred kitten with proper pedigree papers—you might at some future point want to exhibit your cat, after all. Getting a "deal" on an animal without papers will make this difficult and in some cases impossible.

Male, Female, or a Pair of Kittens?

It is, of course, an ideal situation if you can get two kittens at the same time, preferably two littermates, but keep in mind that if you have a male and a female, unless they are neutered there may be kittens. If you are going to have just one cat, it doesn't much matter what sex it is, not even when the time comes to have the animal neutered.

Age of the Cat at Purchase

For someone who has never had a cat, it is simplest to start out with a kitten. A kitten is ready to leave its mother at 12 weeks, and that is when you can pick it up from the breeder. An older cat that is calmer and "better behaved" is preferable in some situations, especially for older people.

A Healthy Kitten

Assess the animal's state of health yourself by watching it carefully. A healthy kitten:
- ✔ is active; likes to play and jump
- ✔ fights with its littermates
- ✔ looks bright and alert
- ✔ eats the food it is given with good appetite
- ✔ purrs when nursing
- ✔ has bright, clear eyes without a trace of tearing
- ✔ has a dry, cool nose
- ✔ gives an overall impression of cleanliness.

TIP

Questions of Your Own
- ✔ What is the age of the kittens?
- ✔ Do they have all their shots yet?
- ✔ What are the prices of the kittens?
- ✔ Why are some different prices?
- ✔ Have they had veterinary inspections?
- ✔ Are the kittens familiar with children and/or dogs?
- ✔ Are the parents registered with CFA?
- ✔ Have the parents been tested free of polycystic kidney disease?
- ✔ Have the parents been shown?
- ✔ May you see the parents?
- ✔ Have the breeders been awarded a *current* Certificate of Cattery Excellence by CFA?
- ✔ Do they have a written guarantee and return policy?

TIP

Determining the Sex
Check for yourself when you buy your kitten to make sure it is the desired sex. You can tell quite easily. In the male, the space between the anus and the genital orifice is larger than in the female; also, the genital orifice is round in males and more slitlike in females. A good analogy is a "period" for a male, and an "exclamation mark" for a female.

A litter of eight-week-old silver kittens. The three kittens to the right are likely to be shaded silver. Note the color on the face above the eyes. The lighter kitten may be the much rarer, and often more expensive chinchilla silver, or simply a small, slower-maturing shaded silver.

This sweet chinchilla silver is rolling over to get a better perspective on a toy just out of camera view.

Very little white on this bi-color means that it will go to a pet home, because the standard calls for more white than this (see page 22). Breeders find this small amount of white pattern is often inherited.

When playing with a rubber ball suspended from an elastic string, a Persian cat practices innate behavior patterns, such as the ones it would use when hunting prey in the wild.

(Look at the animal's rear end. The feces of a healthy cat are solid; only diarrhea leaves traces on the fur. The cat has clean ears without accumulated secretion inside the outer ear. If a cat keeps scratching its ears or shaking its head, this probably means that it has mites or an ear infection.)

Certificate of Cattery Excellence

Ask about the breeder's CFA Certificate of Cattery Excellence. Breeders are very proud of this award and usually post it in a prominent place. Inspected each year by a local veterinarian, the breeder must maintain significantly high standards regarding cleanliness and health of the animals. The Cat Fanciers' Association requires a yearly inspection and renewal. A quick call to CFA will establish whether or not the registration is current.

Formalities of Purchase

Unlike AKC dog breeders, cat breeders are not required by the CFA to give you registration papers or a detailed pedigree upon the purchase of a kitten. They will often withhold the papers and pedigree until you provide written verification from your veterinarian that the kitten has been altered. For this reason, you need to make sure that your written purchase agreement states that your kitten is of pure

TIP

Buying a Cat Abroad

If you buy a cat abroad, the buyer is obliged to give or send you not only pedigree papers and a vaccination certificate but also proof that the animal is entered in the breed register of the country of origin and a document of transfer. If you are getting a cat from some other part of the world, such as Europe or Australia, you can entrust the transport of the animal to an airline without worry. The animals travel in comfortable crates in pressurized cabins. Of course you will have to obtain the necessary documents for entry ahead of time. A permit from the Department of Agriculture is often required, and Customs forms will need to be signed upon delivery.

Persian breeding, and that the papers and pedigree will be given upon proof of neutering.

Registration Papers

The registration papers document that your Persian cat comes of purebred ancestors. They should be issued by a nationally recognized registry, of which the Cat Fanciers' Association is the largest, with many affiliated clubs. Besides authorizing cat shows across the United States, CFA controls a nationwide scoring system for the cat's winnings in its affiliated clubs' shows. CFA also trains and appoints judges, and produces each year a handy CFA *Yearbook*.

It is important to know that there are reciprocal arrangements between the United States' governing bodies for cats and the Canadian Cat Association (CCA), which means that qualified American cats can enter and compete in the Canadian shows, and, of course, vice versa.

If there is any question about registration papers, ask for advice from a cat association. By the way, any official pedigree contains the names and colors of the animal's ancestors four generations back.

Vaccination Certificate

In addition to the pedigree papers, you should be given a vaccination certificate indicating that the animal has received shots

TIP

Buying a Kitten Unseen

The best method of insuring the acquisition of a healthy kitten from other parts of the country is to go there. The minimal cost of flying may save you thousands of dollars in veterinary bills, and allows the kitten to travel with you in the airline cabin.

against distemper, respiratory viruses, and rabies. Cats intended for pedigree breeding are also ready for their first leukemia vaccination.

Purchase Agreement

If you buy a Persian cat, which is an object of considerable financial value, it makes sense to draw up a formal sales agreement. Included in this agreement should be the date of purchase, an exact description of the cat, its sex, vaccinations it has received, the purchase price, and the names and addresses of the buyer and the seller. Don't enter into any special agreements, such as the stipulation that a kitten from the first litter will be accepted as payment, or the breeder will provide free stud service. Many a friendship has been ruined by such informal agreements.

ACCLIMATION AND DAILY LIFE

Imagine being thrown into a new world with no familiar smells and no customary sounds. Where is your family, your mama? The litter pan? In this world of giant strangers where is the soft well-known voice? But wait! That is a familiar smell; it is dinner! And while the voice is not familiar, it is soft and comforting, the arms warm and enveloping.

Arrival at the New Home

Your kitten is entering a world that will bombard it with new sights and sounds. Create a first home for it in a place near your room. Set up the litter pan there, a low one with its usual litter. Create a warm quiet environment, put in a warm bed, use a lamp near its sleeping area, if you are not planning on sleeping together. Never let it be far from a litter pan in those first few days, and never with an adult cat that might block the route to the litter pan and food. And remember, there is plenty of time

It's a big lovely world out there for this adorable tortoiseshell female kitten. Notice her tail feathers have yet to develop, so she is probably only about 14 weeks old. By 10 months of age, this tail fur may be 9 inches (22.5 cm) long, and will be clipped off when she begins breeding.

to introduce it to the children once it has settled into its own room. Christmas and family parties are not the time to parade your new kitten.

Food

Be sure to ask the breeder for some of the kitten's regular food to help carry the baby through the stress of its new household. When you first bring home your new Persian kitten the first step should be to trim back the fur from the back legs and tail base. This will save many hours of bottom baths that often accompany a young kitten under stress from the changes in the household, and works well for older cats that are not being shown.

Adjustment to the New Home

After you have picked up your Persian cat at the breeder's and brought it home in a cat carrier, it has to learn to adjust to its new environment. You should have some food and fresh water ready for it. Put the carrier down in a quiet room in a spot you have decided on beforehand, open the carrier, and wait. After a little while the cat will overcome its fear and, motivated by curiosity, emerge to begin exploring this new territory with cautious and stealthy movements. Some cats immediately hide under an armchair, a cupboard, or a sofa. If that is the case, leave the animal alone and don't try to drag it out by force. Before long, the cat will continue its investigation. For the first few days your Persian cat should stay in one room and get used to it; then you can leave the door open so that it will be able to explore the rest of the house. During this adjustment period the litter box can be kept right next to the carrier.

A solid screen mounted on a wooden frame will keep a cat from escaping or falling out of the window.

What to Have on Hand

Before you bring home your new pet there are a few important items you have to get.

A cat carrier: During the trip home and later for visits to the veterinarian, vacation travel, and journeys to exhibitions, your cat will be most comfortable in an air freight container or in a sleeping basket with a door that locks. Pet supply stores and the pet sections of large department stores sell cat carriers. For use on lengthy trips by car or train, the carrier should be large enough for the cat to stand up and turn around in. Line the bottom with several layers of newspapers and cover the papers with a soft blanket or bath towel.

A sleeping basket: Cats like to sleep in cozy, warm places. Pet supply stores sell cavelike baskets made of foam and soft material that are very practical. Indoors, you can take the door off, and have the carrier serve as a bed. When the door is hooked in place and locked, the carrier can function as a retreat that the cat knows and feels safe in.

Food and water dishes: Always have dry cat food and water available for your cats. Use heavy earthenware bowls that are not easily pushed around or knocked over. Food dishes glazed on the inside and designed for rabbits (available at pet supply stores) are also practical and inexpensive. Serve wet food such as meat, canned cat food, and warm cereal on discardable plates, or in heavy glass, or sturdy ceramic bowls, because they are easy to clean and can be put in the microwave if the food needs to be warmed up. Plastic dishes cannot be adequately cleaned, and they hold odors.

A litter box: Various kinds of litter boxes are sold at pet supply stores. The most practical are those with a top and a removable drawer for the litter. This design prevents the litter from flying out when the cat scratches in it to bury the feces. Pour a layer of about 1½ to 2 inches (3–5 cm) of cat litter in the bottom.

The litter suppresses odors and should absorb moisture well. There is no need to clean out the box every day; just remove the feces and the spots of wet litter with a small trowel and fill the holes with new litter. Once a week you should wash the box thoroughly with hot water. The safest disinfectant to use with cats is simple chlorine bleach; do not use other varieties as these contain other ingredients such as lye, which leaves an irritating residue. The phenolic compounds readily poison cats, so steer clear of any cleanser with an "ol" at the end of the ingredients, such as phenol.

Cats are very sensitive to smells and may refuse to use a box if it has an offensive odor. A litter box like the one just described doesn't work for kittens less than eight weeks old because the entrance is too high. A plastic pan about 12 by 24 inches (30 × 60 cm) and with a rim about 2 inches (5 cm) high is better. The litter box should be kept in a permanent, out-of-the-way place. The bathroom is fine, but the box must always be accessible to the cat.

An object for scratching: Persians, just like any other cats, need to sharpen their claws. To keep your upholstered furniture as safe from cats' claws as possible, you should offer your cat a more attractive alternative. The pet supply industry offers a variety of choices: cat carpets, special scratching paper, scratching posts (see above right), scratching and climbing trees, and even trees with shelves for sleeping on; they are sold in many different versions and in various price ranges. If you like to make things yourself, you can construct your own scratching tree. Just

Cats have a natural need to sharpen their claws. To keep them from using the furniture for this purpose, you should supply a sturdy scratching post. Sisal rope is the best choice.

make sure that it is sturdy—your cat will never again touch a scratching tree that topples over the first time it is used. Cats seem to prefer sisal rope posts over carpeted posts.

Cat-proofing windows and balconies: An open window or a balcony harbors several dangers for your Persian cat. Prevent escape or falling out of a window by installing a relatively simple safety screen. Stretch sturdy wire mesh over a wooden frame that fits into the window opening and lock it in place with two bolts attached to the window frame (see drawing on page 38). However, such a screen is no deterrent to breaking and entering and therefore not adequate for ground floor windows. Pet supply stores have safety nets for balconies with easy-to-follow instructions for installation.

Note: Casement windows can turn into deadly traps if a cat gets caught in one.

This low-sided litter pan is perfect for a young kitten. But with that adult sitting on top, a new kitten may be too intimidated to approach the litter pan. Solution? Put a couple of laundry baskets, on the shelves above, eliminating the overview.

Cat toys: Pet stores and cat boutiques sell a great variety of cat toys. Cats like balls of crumpled paper that rustle when batted around just as well; they also play with old tennis and table tennis balls and crocheted wool mice, and they like to roll around inside empty, well-washed, round laundry soap tubs.

Scratch resistant furniture: Velveteen or other tight-thread furniture may survive years with your cat. Sofas and chairs with nubby or looped threads are sure to fall quick victim to enthusiastic cat scratching.

An Ideal Indoor Cat

Most Persian cats are kept indoors. This does not mean that their natural needs are ignored or squelched; it assures them a long, happy, and safe life. But even indoors, the hazards can be significant, from disinfectants used on the floors, to tinsel hanging from the Christmas tree, to an aspirin dropped on the carpet.

Spending Time Outside

Because of their long fur and the grooming this fur requires, Persian cats are not well suited for outdoor life. There is nothing wrong, however, with occasional brief outings to the garden or yard, as long as they are supervised. However, the animal should be completely familiar with its new home before it is allowed out for the first time. When the cat is ready, let it venture out, perhaps through an open terrace door, on its first tentative investigation of the outside world. The outdoors, of course, holds many dangers (accidents, sources of infection) to an unsuspecting Persian cat. If you have a garden, you can set up an outdoor run for your cat that is escape-proof. The best kind of grating to use is hardware cloth, and there should be a little door through which the animal can get back into the house anytime it wants to. There are cat doors commercially available that are easy to install in any normal door.

Note: When I say "outdoor run" I do not mean a pen in which the cat is kept all the

A copper-eyed white kitten. Imagine trying to take sticky maple leaves and burrs from this coat if the cat gets outside. Keeping the feet and ruff white is a daily show chore.

time. Persian cats always have to have regular contact with people!

Leash: With some patience on their owner's part, many Persian cats can be trained—preferably when they are still young—to walk on a leash and harness (see drawing on right). A leash is also a good deterrent against escape when you carry your Persian cat.

With a little patience, almost any Persian cat can be taught to walk on a leash. A leash is also useful when you carry your cat on your arm on a walk; it serves as an extra precaution against escape.

List of Dangers (Indoors and Outdoors)

Source	Effects	Precautions
Balcony	Danger of falling.	Enclose your balcony (nets are commercially available for this purpose).
Iron	Burning nose when sniffing; pulling cord and knocking iron down.	Don't leave cat alone in a room with a hot iron.
Electric wires	Chewing through the wires, electrocution.	Thread cords through PVC pipe to prevent cord chewing.
Windows	Escaping; falling from great height; getting caught in casement window (very common!).	Install sturdy wire screening; never leave casement window ajar.
Firecrackers	Firecrackers can cause deafness or shock from fright if they are set off too close to a cat; a firecracker can explode inside the mouth if a cat chews on it.	Don't set off fireworks yourself. Shut windows and don't leave cat alone on holidays when fireworks are displayed; stay home and reassure your cat.
Burners of stove	Cat can burn paws if it jumps onto hot burners.	Place covers on burners; don't leave the cat alone in the kitchen.
Candles	Knocking over a burning candle; danger of a fire.	Do without candlelight.
Tinsel	The glitter tempts cats to catch tinsel, which may be swallowed and is indigestible.	Do without tinsel.
Sewing needles	Can be swallowed; threaded needles are especially dangerous.	Be very careful with sewing accessories; don't leave them lying around.
Antifreeze, oil, phenol (engine and heating oil)	These contain substances that are toxic to cats; can be dangerous on contact.	This danger often can't be avoided because cats like to sit under cars.
Plants	Injuries or poisoning.	Don't keep poisonous plants or cacti indoors or on balcony. Find out what plants are poisonous.

List of Dangers (Indoors and Outdoors) (continued)

Source	Effects	Precautions
Plastic bags	Cats like to crawl into them, can get caught inside and suffocate.	Don't leave plastic bags lying around.
Cupboards	Kittens can get caught behind or underneath them or climb up too high and get hurt jumping down.	Keep young kittens (less than 12 weeks old) with their mother in the room where they were born; their safety depends on your vigilance.
Chairs	Paws can get stuck in ornamental decorations of wooden or wrought iron chairs.	This does not happen with plain chairs.
Tablecloths	Catching a claw when reaching up from the floor, pulling tablecloth down and getting burned by hot soup, coffee, or tea.	Place mats don't stick out over the edge of the table and are therefore not likely to be pulled down.
Doors	Getting squashed by a closing door; escaping; being locked in or out.	Only careful watching can prevent escape and accidents.
Washing machine	Accidentally locking the cat in a front-loading machine.	Caution: never leave the door open; reach into the machine before each use to make sure no cat is inside.
Detergents, cleansers, chemicals	Poisoning; acid burns from licking or accidental contact.	Keep all household cleansers locked away in cupboards.
Yarn, rubber bands	Getting entangled; wrapping yarn or rubber band around paws or neck.	Don't offer balls of yarn or rubber bands for playing; tie toys to ribbons and suspend them about 4 inches (10 cm) above the ground.
Cigarettes	Burns; nicotine poisoning from eating the tobacco.	It would be best to give up smoking; otherwise use ashtrays with covers.

Brown tabby beauties. The kitten on the right has widely separated eyes, while the kitten on the left has better striping. Six of eight judges will likely pick the "eyes" (30 points on head) over the stripes (20 points on color).

This black-and-white bi-color shows wonderful show grooming, even on the belly and between the front legs. The judge may mention that, when grooming, a cat has more than a topside to it! This is often a not-so-subtle message that he or she just found a little belly mat.

This solid black has poor eye color, but fantastic small ears.

A solid cream or cream tabby? This young cat may have some problem with its lack of a full coat, which might disguise some of those leg stripes. Likely some judge is going to switch it from solid cream to cream tabby, and the next judge back from cream tabby to solid cream.

When a young Persian is learning to balance properly in the litter pan, it frequently fails to make the transition from squat to standing. And when the fur is particularly long, or you succumbed to giving it that dish of cream, messy bottoms are an inevitable result. A bottom bath is almost always the result of failure to clip off the bottom fur, or strange foods upsetting the delicate intestinal tract. Curiously, this is often the one reason, *not* often stated, as to why people do not want to deal with a Persian.

Temperature

Your kitten is most comfortable at about 90°F (32.2°C). This is why it loves being in your arms, next to your face, or in your hair at night. If you are going to give your kitten a bottom bath, recognize its need for heat.

Steps

✔ First turn on the bathroom heater to keep the kitten from becoming chilled while you work. If you lack a bathroom heater, turn on all the lights for a couple of hours. If it is hot weather,

turn off the air conditioning or at least close the vents into the bathroom. A cold kitten is a kitten in danger.

✔ A bottom bath consists of carefully working free any fecal matter, with toilet or facial tissues. If very messy you might want to do this over the toilet bowl or into a bucket you designate for this and not for any other purpose such as household cleaning. After freeing most of the discharge, fill the sink with warm water and carefully wash the kitten's bottom. No soap is needed for this, and may, in fact, aggravate the diarrhea.

✔ Once the water runs clear, you may use some baby shampoo to freshen the scent. Rinse, rinse, rinse until the fur is squeaky-clean. Then towel the kitten dry.

✔ Take a warm but not hot blow-dryer to the bottom and gently finish blowing dry.

Blow-drying

Your kitten's first bottom bath can cause some permanent damage if you have a kitten that is going to get scared by the sound of the blow-dryer. Be prepared with first aid and towels.

Blow-drying is begun after towel-drying, with a comb to

Make sure when you bathe your Persian cat that its head stays dry.

A BOTTOM BATH

lift and separate the hair in order to speed the drying process. There are noisy blow-dryers and quiet ones. Experiment with each to determine which one is bearable to the kitten.

At the beginning of blow-drying, wrap the kitten securely in your towel, then turn on the blow-dryer. If the kitten begins to behave frantically, hold it securely in your arms, still wrapped tightly in the towel, and turn away from the blow-dryer. Then turn slowly toward the blow-dryer with the bottom of the kitten first, its head away from the dryer. If it is still impossible to dry the kitten, turn off the blow-dryer and place the kitten in a carrier. Turn the blow-dryer on low heat and low speed. Every ten minutes, turn off the blow-dryer, remove the kitten, and comb gently through the coat. Place the kitten back in the carrier and turn the dryer back on. Never leave any cat unattended with a blow-dryer.

Carrier Grill Bottom

Try to buy a carrier with a grill insert bottom. Take four cans of cat food and place them under the grill. This will raise the grill flooring so that the air will also dry the underside of the cat.

Bite Wounds

Always keep on hand hydrogen peroxide and Epsom salts. These are your own bathing and drying first aid items. If you are bitten by the kitten, immediately pour hydrogen peroxide on the wound, until it stops bubbling. Then immerse the wound in an Epsom salt warm water soak for at least ten minutes, every couple of hours. Repeat the hydrogen peroxide no more than once every 24 hours. This should prevent infections.

Bottom Baths
- Heat the bathroom to 90°F (32.2°C).
- Shut the air conditioning off, or block vent.
- Collect
  - Disposable latex gloves
  - Warm towels
  - Baby shampoo
  - A low-sided bucket or dishpan
  - Hair dryer
- Put on disposable gloves.
- Work feces free.
- Rinse in warm water.
- Empty bucket or sink.
- Repeat until water is clear.
- Remove gloves.
- Shampoo and rinse.
- Rinse again. And again.
- Towel-dry.
- Finish with warm blow-dryer.

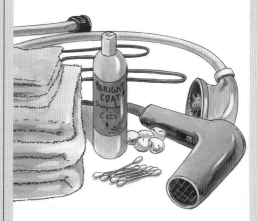

Persians will not naturally gravitate toward the foods that are best for them. The result, at the best of times, will be diarrhea from milk. At the worst of times, it will be liver, kidney, or heart damage from an improper diet.

How a Cat Eats

You can tell from watching the way a Persian cat eats—even if it has never seen, let alone caught, killed, and consumed, a mouse—that cats are hunters. Pieces of meat the size of a mouse are eaten right away only if the cat is very hungry. Otherwise, they are pulled off the plate, dragged around, tossed into the air, swallowed whole without chewing, regurgitated, sometimes hidden. Even tiny kittens defend their "prey" by growling and spitting at their siblings. Mushy or liquid food, on the other hand, which is not part of a cat's natural diet, is eaten out of the same bowl by several cats together without any conflict over the food.

Commercial Cat Food

The advantages of commercial cat food are obvious. It can be stored in the form it will be given, it doesn't spoil, it can be taken along on trips, and it contains everything a cat needs to stay healthy. The proportions of protein, fat, carbohydrates, vitamins, and trace elements are designed to match those found in the prey cats would eat in the wild.

Canned cat food: This is made up of meat (muscle meat, heart, liver, lung), cereals (rice, barley, wheat, corn), and vegetables and yeast. It comes in various flavors, such as beef, poultry, game, and fish. If you want to know the exact composition of different brands you can study and compare the labels. Canned cat food usually contains 70 to 80 percent water; 10 to 14 percent protein; about 5 percent fat; 5 percent carbohydrates; plus vitamins, minerals, and trace elements. Some canned foods, consisting primarily of meat, have less carbohydrates.

Dry cat food: Just like canned cat food, dry cat food is nutritionally complete; in other words, you can feed your cat exclusively on dry cat food. It, too, comes in different flavors. Unlike canned food, dry cat food has only about 15 percent water, so the cat has to drink more water if you feed it mostly dry food. Dry cat food is more highly concentrated than the canned version and therefore goes farther. You don't need to give your cat as much of it to satisfy its need for calories.

Keep dry food available at all times, especially for kittens.

Feeding Dishes

1 A flat disposable plate for soft food, ceramic bowls for dry food, and a deep bowl for fresh water are the simplest of your Persian's needs.

2 The flat plate helps with the flat face, and meticulous need to keep the whiskers clean.

3 The deep bowl with a narrow top will help prevent a perennially wet chin.

4 Do not use plastic; it will not sanitize readily, causing chin acne or the passing of diseases from one cat to another.

Note: Commercial dog food is cheaper that commercial cat food. Often, people who have both dogs and cats ask me if dog food is not just as good as cat food. The answer is that dog food contains considerably less protein, and if you give it to a cat over an extended period of time, your cat will not be properly nourished.

Cooking for Your Cat

Although commercial cat food contains everything that is essential for proper feline nutrition, many cat owners like to give their pets something home cooked now and then. There are elaborate charts with scientifically calculated numbers indicating how much of each food element, vitamin, and so forth a cat needs, and with a whole week's worth of cat menus. But you can cook for your Persian cat much more simply and still feed it a healthy diet.

Muscle meat bought at the butcher's is the most important source of protein for cats. The best kinds of meat given raw are horse meat, rabbit, chicken, and turkey. (Poultry hearts and gizzards are especially popular because they are inexpensive!) Beef and pork always have to be cooked first because they may contain pathogens (possible danger of Aujeszky's disease, toxoplasmosis, and worms.

Organ meats (other than poultry heart and gizzard) are often cheap, too, but have to be cooked. Liver, if eaten raw, causes diarrhea and tends to constipate when cooked. Cats usually like heart, which should be fed in mouse-size pieces so that the cat can strengthen its chewing muscles. Lung is cheap but not particularly nutritious, and cats are not especially fond of it. It has to be cut very small or pureed. If you have a neutered cat that is overweight, you can try mixing some pureed liver with its ordinary food. Liver tends to cause diarrhea, and tripe is too tough for cats to handle well.

Bones of large animals are useless to cats, and poultry bones that have been cooked are too dangerous because they splinter easily and may get stuck between the teeth or in the throat.

Fish is very popular with many cats. It should be cooked and deboned; inexpensive filets of ocean fish are suitable.

Hard cheese, grated fine, can be sprinkled over the food—but only now and then as a special treat.

The yolk of a raw egg is another treat cats like. You can give one to your cat two or three times a week, but make sure you give the yolk only; the egg white destroys the B vitamins in the food.

Potatoes, rice, noodles, oatmeal, barley, a taste of vegetable—all of them cooked—can occasionally be added to a cat's food, about ⅔ to 1 ounce (20–30 g) at a time. Here it is a good idea to put the entire meal in the blender first so that the cat won't pick out the pieces of meat and leave the rest.

Yeast flakes (about 1 teaspoon per day) as well as vitamin and mineral supplements (available at pet supply stores) should always be added to homemade meals.

A Tip: Ailing kittens like to lick up a gruel made of 3 tablespoons instant baby oatmeal, 1 teaspoon yeast flakes, 1 egg yolk, and 1 cup diluted canned milk (don't sweeten it!). Be sure to watch the cat's stool, however; milk can give cats diarrhea (see page 78).

Proper Feeding

Be strict about what you give your Persian cat to eat, and don't spoil it by letting it have steak, ham, or chicken all the time. If you keep making exceptions, you encourage your cat to approach its regular meals without enthusiasm, and soon it will never be really satiated or really hungry.

The feeding place should not be changed around continually. A cat likes to eat in peace in a familiar place. Wash the food and water dishes with hot water after every meal.

The feeding should always be done by the same person, if possible.

Regular feeding times are important. The best time is just before or during your own meal times. Adult cats should be fed once or twice a day; younger cats, two to four times a day.

When drinking, a cat curls its tongue down and backward, then dips it into the water or milk to lap it up.

═══════════════════
■■■■ T I P ■■■■
═══════════════════

Amount to Feed

Give your cat as much to eat as it seems to want. If there are leftovers, give a little less next time. Cats that are still growing, pregnant cats, or nursing mothers cannot be overfed. If you have an older neutered cat, feed it some its less favorite foods now and then on a regular basis.

Old cats should be given their daily food ration distributed over a number of smaller meals, and, if they have lost their teeth, the food should be pureed. Pregnant or nursing mother cats should always have fresh food available.

Amounts of Food

It is impossible to prescribe amounts that would suit all cats. The requirements of different animals vary. As a general guideline, the daily amount of food needed by a cat that is under no special

A cream point Himalayan, with excellent eye color.

A flame point Himalayan, also called a red point.

A rainbow litter! Crossing a blue-cream with a red male leads to a wonderful array of kitten colors.

This water bowl is too wide. Use a narrow china bowl shaped like a coffee mug.
China rather than plastic is preferred, to prevent chin acne.

A long adult coat will hide the tall ears on this playful kitten, while sexual maturity may
develop a wider head and will likely bring up the nose.

54

physical stress, such as the growth of youth, pregnancy, nursing, or mating, lies between about
.65 to .8 ounces of food per pound of body weight
(40–50 g per 1 kg). This would mean that about 6
to 7 ounces of canned cat food would be enough
for a cat weighing about 9 pounds (200 g for a
cat weighing 4 kg). The same guidelines apply to
homemade meals, assuming the composition is
varied enough. If you make up your cat's meals
yourself, you should always change the main
ingredients several times a week. If you give your
cat primarily dry cat food (see page 49), about
2¾ ounces (80 g) a day is enough. A ten-year-old,
large, and muscular Persian stud who weighs
12 pounds (5½ kg) gets 2½ to 2¾ ounces (70–
80 g; 2 handsful) of dry cat food a day.

Obesity

Like most creatures, cats vary a great deal in
their food likes and dislikes, eating habits, effi-
ciency of food conversion, body size, temperament, and number of fat cells produced. There
are cats that, because of their physical consti-
tution, start putting on layers of fat when
weighing no more than 6 or 7 pounds (3 kg),
whereas others have hardly an ounce of fat
on them even though they weight 13 pounds
(6 kg). When one considers other factors that
may endanger a cat's life, obesity and its possible negative effects on health and longevity
don't seem to me to merit excessive concern.
I have seen many cats that have enjoyed good
health over many years and continued eating
with great relish whatever leftover food they
could get—in spite of being on the heavy side.
If you can manage to keep your cat at its ideal
weight without too much trouble, you should
do so by all means.

What Should a Persian Cat Drink?

Water: Cats always have to have fresh water
available. Change the water every day, and
offer it in a clean bowl. Cats that are given
dry cat food have a particular need for as
much water as they like. Many cats prefer to
get their water from a flower vase. There is
no need to worry about this, as long as there
is always fresh water available at the feeding
place.

Milk: Canned milk is an excellent source of
protein and calcium for a nursing mother cat.
If you give a nursing mother cat milk mixed
with egg yolk and instant cereal, the kittens
will thrive especially well. Milk agrees with
many cats, but it does cause diarrhea in some.
It is the lactose in the milk that has this effect
on the digestive system. You can use milk to
normalize your cat's digestion if needed, giving
it to counteract constipation and withdrawing
it if there is diarrhea.

Milk Allergies

Milk is a frequent cause of diarrhea in
Persians who are often unable to process cows'
milk. If you must give milk, try diluted canned
milk or goats' milk. You will likely find, though,
the pleasure of giving a comforting cup of milk
is hardly matched by what goes on several
hours later from the rear!

Do Persian Cats Need to Eat Grass?

Most Persian cats like to nibble on "something green," and I consider grass important
for cats, especially Persian cats. You can

Is Your Persian Too Thin or Too Fat?

Appearance	Flanks (thigh)	Ribs	Backbone	Upper hips	Neck	Tummy tuck up in front of hips
Thin	No fat	Ribs visible	Backbone visible	Hip bones prominent	Neck bones and hyoid prominent	Prominent
Underweight	Minimal fat	Ribs easily felt	Vertebrae easily felt	Hip bones easily felt	Neck bones and hyoid easily felt	Easily felt
Ideal	Flank folds obvious	Palpable, ribs not visible	Backbone not visible	Hip bones not visible	Neck bones and hyoid no longer felt	Full waist, but folds empty in front of hips
Overweight	Folds have some sway	Some fat obscuring ribs	Backbone has some fat overlay	Hip bones have some fat overlay	Neck bones not felt	Waist folds in front of hips drooping with some fat
Obese	Folds sway significantly, often with rolling gait	Ribs hard to feel	Backbone hard to find	Hip bones covered with fat rolls	Neck no longer distinguishable from shoulders	Waist folds impede straight-forward gait

buy small flats with grass growing in them at pet supply stores or sow some grass seed in a flowerpot. After eating grass, cats often choke it up again together with hair they have swallowed in the course of licking themselves. This regurgitation may be accompanied by noises and coughs that can sound most alarming.

To prevent the formation of hair balls in the stomach, as well as to aid the passage of hair through the digestive system, you can give your cat medicines containing Vaseline (available at pet supply stores). Let your cat lick a bit of butter or margarine off your finger now and then. This is regarded as a treat by the cat and at the same time helps the cat's digestion.

PERSIAN PERSONALITY AND BEHAVIOR

The Persian communicates with chirps and soft squeaky cries. You may find yourself carrying on an extensive conversation with the Persian, since they often signal, "Where are you, Mom?" "My water dish needs changing," or even "Mind if I join you in the tub?" Your Persian will follow you everywhere, and is often the solution to the Empty Nest Syndrome.

When playful, Persians may dig into the trash to find a crumpled piece of paper, bringing it to you with a beckoning cry. Dropping the paper at your feet, they will attempt to teach to you the game of Fetch. Cry *"Fetch,"* and throw the paper, and the cat will fetch it back until it becomes bored. Sadly, you will likely become bored before the cat, so don't be surprised when it reappears with a fresh piece of paper from the trashcan. This inherited Persian tendency to fetch seems to be related to the instinct to bring prey back to the nest and teach the youngsters to hunt, but is readily molded into the game called "Fetch" by humans.

The natural black eye liner, required on silvers, is commonly called "mascara," and should also outline the lips and nose.

Teaching a Persian Its Name

A Persian is easily taught its name, much faster than dogs. Call the cat's name, immediately scratch its back near the tail. Call the name again, and again, quickly scratch the rump. By the third time, the kitten will likely twirl on tiptoes in response to the name. Keep reinforcing this name every few days, with the positive scratching on the back, just as a reminder. If you have two Persian kittens, you will be amazed at the speed they will learn their own names, compared to puppies.

If you have more than one Persian, be sure to have fairly different call names, such as a Topper and a Whopper. Call one "Top-Top" and the other Whopper. This will help considerably

Body postures of a Persian cat.

Self-confidence and attention.

Uncertainty—shying back.

Defensive readiness to give way.

Fear—readiness for self-defense.

when you want Top-Top to stop scratching the furniture or to have a treat. Never call your Persian "Kitty." These are friendly cats to begin with, and you do not want them walking away with strangers. Even visitors to your home should be told to call them by their names, and watch the cat come strolling up to be petted.

Behavior

Cats are individualists. They will not put up with being drilled, and they cannot be taught "manners" the way it is successfully done with dogs through obedience training. But that doesn't mean that cats are incapable of learning or that their behavior cannot be influenced. Cats have acute senses, a great capacity for understanding, and a sensitive soul. If you take the time and patience to "convince" a cat of the usefulness of doing or not doing certain things, it will often behave the way you want it to of its own accord. Probably the most important ingredients for success in such educational attempts are love for the animal, patience, consistency, authority, and repetition—rewards but no punishment. Shouting won't do any good with a Persian cat.

Painless Playing

Persians are inherently gentle, but also very sensitive to their owner's moods and needs, and can readily learn not to bite hard. Lively, spirited cats and, above all, kittens, love wild play, and a human partner is a favorite playmate. The cat will chase after balls of crumpled paper with delight, try to pounce on a ball that is pulled along on a string, and sometimes even fetch a toy in the manner of a canine retriever. To keep the cat's hunting instinct from taking on an undesirable aspect, and to avoid being bitten or scratched, you should not use your hand as an "object of play." Always have a variety of feathered toys on sticks nearby, or long pheasant feathers. These will fit readily into the bedside drawer or desk, and quickly teaches your kitten where the goodies are kept.

When your kitten or cat grabs your hand to play with it, cry out softly. Persians are usually responsive and will lighten up the biting. If this does not work, try blowing on its face, or tapping on the top of the offending paw; both of these techniques are far more effective with Persians than yelling *"No!"*

Scratching the Furniture

Yelling generally results in simply identifying what your Persians need to do to gain your attention, so they will race off with their ears laid back, only to return later to repeat this newfound yelling game. If the *"No!"* was meant to prevent them from scratching the furniture, a far more effective ploy is a spray bottle of water. Without making a sound, when your Persian scratches the furniture, silently spray the cat with water. Then when you leave the house, it will be less likely to scratch the furniture, since it associates the behavior more with the water spray, and less with your presence. Persians may be bright cats, but they are not rocket scientists. If they still insist on scratching, fold tin foil over the arms and sides of the chair. Then, remove it when company comes. This also works well on kitchen surfaces.

Declawing

If you are reluctant to attempt regular monthly nail clipping, your veterinarian can

TIP

Spending Time with Your Cat

Persian cats, most of which are kept indoors almost exclusively, need affection and physical closeness from their owners. Cats kept singly and without sufficient attention from their owners show signs of this deprivation in their behavior; some become nervous and shy, others, apathetic or aggressive. Also, animals that are not happy get sick more easily and their cleanliness may deteriorate. If you don't have much time or will be able to devote yourself to your cat only occasionally, you should not keep one cat in an apartment but should get two instead.

introduce you to special silicone nail covers that need replacing every few months. Declawing is not recommended, and in fact, in some countries it is considered inhumane and illegal to surgically declaw cats.

"Conversations"

Some cats regularly and almost predictably "answer" with a conversational squeak when spoken to, looking attentively at the person who is talking. These "conversations" help establish and strengthen a strong bond between the cat and its human friend.

Petting

Persian cats love being petted. They express their enjoyment by purring, cooing, reaching up their heads for more, snuggling up to people, and often—when very relaxed—by kneading. Some cats also retain an infantile behavior trait even into old age, namely, sucking on your thumb or on the inside of your elbow.

Running into the street: It is possible to "spoil" specific places for cats. This is done quite simply by linking the forbidden place with unpleasant experiences. When I noticed, for instance, that an outdoor cat of mine liked to run into the street, I started hitting the asphalt of the sidewalk with a cane every time I saw the cat approach. This cat is still alive today, having lived in the garden and barn for 16 years without accidents, and it stays away from the street. It may take a long time before a cat starts to respect your wishes. No matter how long it takes, you will have to repeat the discouraging action you have settled on over and over again every time you notice the cat running in the forbidden direction.

Adding a Second Cat

Cats live in a pride structure similar to that of lions. A new adult is seldom ever welcome, unless of the opposite sex, and new kittens may find themselves living on the edge of the main territory, blocked from food and litter pan simply by a bold stare. Regardless, statistics show that cat owners are likely to have multiple cats, so it is almost inevitable that you will find yourself at some point introducing a new cat or kitten.

If you have to be away from home a good part of the day, you would be better off getting two cats. The animals will form a close bond, act out some of their natural social behavior with each other, and thus will be less affected by the periods when they have to do without human company. Ideally, the two Persian cats can be introduced and get used to each other while they are still kittens.

An "old" cat and a kitten: Even when an adult cat has been living alone with its family for some time, you can still, in almost all situations, introduce a new kitten into the household. During the adjustment period, when there is bound to be considerable spitting and some occasional striking out with the claws, the old cat has a special need to have its owners demonstrate their continuing affection for it. After a few days it usually accepts the innocently playful newcomer, and often the two cats develop a close friendship.

Two "old" cats: It is a little harder to get two grown Persian cats to accept each other; you have to introduce them to each other gradually and with great patience. It is best if they first see and smell each other separated by bars or wire mesh. During this phase, the already established cat always should be treated with special consideration. Cats are individualists, and their reactions are hard to predict. Sometimes, two adult cats very soon start living together in peaceful harmony. In other cases, it takes ages for friendly toleration to develop, if ever. If it doesn't, you should try to find another home for the "new" cat.

Driving with a Persian Cat

Different cats respond differently to riding in a car. As a general rule, kittens adjust more quickly to this form of locomotion than older cats. Place your cat in its carrier and then in the car calmly and without nervousness. The unaccustomed noises will be upsetting to the animal at first. Talking to it soothingly may help, though most cats do best if the carrier is placed in the backseat, and secured with a seat belt.

Never take the cat out of its carrier while driving. Many cats have been killed after being slammed into the dashboard or windshield during an unexpected stop. A number of cats sleep quietly most of the time in the car; others keep complaining vociferously, trying to attract your attention. Never leave a cat or any other living creature alone in the car when the temperature is over 50°F (10°C); even on a cloudy day there is a rapid buildup of heat.

Note: A general rule of thumb—if you close up a car on a sunny day, you may expect a 50-degree rise in temperature within 15 minutes.

Sexual Behavior

Around the age of eight months, though sometimes as early as five months, Persians begin to exhibit some unusual behavior. The females will begin to coo and rub up against anything that holds still. Males will begin grabbing your forearm and straddling it with their back legs. They may even begin to back up to the drapes, releasing small quantities of urine—very smelly urine. Unless you plan on entertaining your neighbors for several houses around, now is the time to neuter your male or spay your female.

Neutering

Most veterinarians are now willing to neuter kittens as early as four months of age. An animal that is neutered has its hormone-producing organs removed by means of surgery (under anesthesia). In the case of a male cat, these organs are the testes; in a female, they are the ovaries. Any cat that is not intended for pedigreed breeding should be neutered. Because no more sexual hormones are produced after the operation, the unpleasant manifestations of the sexual drive (crying, spraying urine, restlessness) are eliminated along with the animal's desire to satisfy sexual needs. Neutering in no way affects the well-being of a cat, whether male or female.

Present veterinary studies on long-term health effects of early neutering show that a *tomcat* should be neutered before reaching sexual maturity—at 8 to 10 months. It does not develop problems urinating later on. Older toms can be neutered at any time with no negative effects, though hormone therapy may be needed to reduce the habit of territorial spraying.

A *female cat* should also be neutered—or spayed as it is usually called in females—before 10 months. But the cat should not be in heat at the time. Older cats that have had several litters can still be spayed. It is not true, as many people think, that a cat should have had at least one litter before it is neutered.

After the operation, which is usually a matter of routine surgery, you are allowed to take your cat home again. As long as the animal is still under the influence of the anesthetic it should be watched and kept warm.

Sterilization

This kind of operation does not affect the hormone-producing glands of the animal; instead, the spermatic cords (in the male) or the oviducts (in the female) are severed. Consequently, sexual hormones continue to be formed even though the animal is sterile and can no longer produce offspring. Sterilization has no advantages whatsoever over neutering because it does not stop any of the annoying manifestations of sexual behavior in either male or female cats. That is why you should have your Persian cat fully neutered rather than sterilized.

If the Cat Refuses to Use the Litter Box

Cats are clean animals by nature and normally use the litter box without prompting. It is very rare for a cat to urinate or defecate in other places in the apartment. If this behavior is not caused by sickness or some understandable psychological reason (a move to a different apartment, for instance, or new members in the household, human or animal), you should try placing several new cat boxes in places the cat seems to favor. Then you have to try, persistently, to make improper spots unattractive by covering over the odor (spraying them with perfume) and to discourage the unacceptable behavior. Often, sexually motivated scent marking is regarded as a bad habit, but it is perfectly normal behavior in a sexually mature animal. Male cats are especially given to marking, and living in an apartment with a tomcat that sprays is intolerable. The best and only solution is to have the cat altered.

Once your veterinarian has determined there is no veterinary emergency due to kidney or bladder problems, you should consider other reasons.

New Litter

Quite often the problem is as simple as suddenly introducing a new brand of litter. Cats are sensitive to change, and may not relate the new litter as the acceptable alternative! For that reason, introduce litter changes gradually. Combine a small amount of the new litter each day with the old, until by the end of the week, only the new litter is being used.

Correcting Poor Litter Pan Habits

✔ Scoop litter daily.
✔ Did you introduce a new litter?
✔ Change weekly or more often?
✔ Does each cat have its own pan?
✔ Did you move the pan?
✔ Did you change the household routine?
✔ Is the pan the correct depth?
✔ Kittens' pans should be 2–3 inches (5–7 cm) high; adults' pans 5–7 inches (13–18 cm) high.

Restrict the Cat

The first step is to restrict the cat or kitten back to its old territory, preferably the bathroom or laundry room.

Divide Territories

The cat or kitten should not compete for territory with another cat. Sometimes the problem is readily solved by dividing the household into several territories, one for

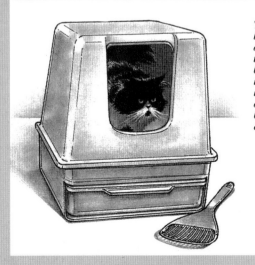

This type of litter box design keeps the litter from being kicked into the room when the cat digs in it to bury its excrements.

each cat, with its pan, food, and water area, with the family room being mutually exclusive of all these.

Caging the Cat

In extreme cases you may need to cage the cat, with its pan, food, and water, which creates a very small territory indeed. Release it to join the family in the evening and then recage it at night or when the family is gone during the day. Always leave the door of the cage open so that the cat feels it can safely return to eat and eliminate within its own territory.

Missing the Litter Pan

Quite often, a litter pan that is adequate for a kitten will not be high enough to prevent the adult cat from hanging its rump over the side. If you have not already done so, now would be a good time to get one of the hooded litter pans.

Sadly, some fastidious cats prefer a more open pan where odors are not trapped. These require the very large, high-sided litter pans that appear to take about 20 pounds of litter at a time. Do not fill these high-sided pans in that fashion, because the cat is once again sitting high with its rear over the side! Instead, take your least favorite newspaper editorial section, fold it carefully, and line the bottom of the pan. Drop about six to eight cups of litter on the newspaper. The next day, wrap up the litter in the newsprint and toss it away! This not only saves lots of deposits on the pan, but can give you the immense satisfaction of venting your frustration at the editorial page in a positive fashion.

Potted-Plant Litter Pans

Occasionally, a cat or kitten will find to its delight that it does not have to go all the way back to the laundry room to accomplish its business, not when there is a perfectly good

Sometimes progesterone pills will stop inappropriate urination (if due to territorial marking), especially in adult males that are neutered later in life.

litter pan sitting in the corner of the living room. There goes another potted palm. Go to the garden shop and buy one of the cheap bags of large-sized river rocks; stack a few around the base of your potted plant, thus discouraging this behavior.

Elderly Cats

During the last years of a cat's life, it may simply give up on the litter pan altogether. Aging cats become forgetful and even incontinent. You may find that "stud pants" may be used instead of caging up the poor old dear. These small-sized plastic panties used to prevent female dogs from being mated may be purchased at any pet store. A small sanitary napkin is placed inside, to be changed several times a day. From the name, you may also deduce that they are usually used to allow spraying males to visit in the house.

GROOMING AND PHYSICAL CARE

Some recognize spring by the arrival of crocus and almond blossoms, the Persian-owning household by the appearance of fine fur wafting through the air. This is the start of the twice yearly molting— the major molt is in April, the summer molt in August. Trousers, the car seat, even the coffee cup at the office will reflect the errant cat hair.

Molting

All cat owners have two choices when their cat is molting—either invest in those clothes that match the colors of your Persians' coats, or deal with the Persian's coat. Most recommended for clothing are various polyesters and other smooth fabrics. Dealing with the cat's shedding is the more reasonable course.

Types of Fur

The Persian coat is like all cat's coats consisting of three separate types of fur. There are the long, sparse, hard, pointed hairs, which are known as "guard hairs." There are finer hairs, nearly as long, that give the Persian coat the length and beauty. Careful breeding has produced a third type of coat hair to its fullest, the wooly undercoat. All Persians have this wooly undercoat to differing extents.

At times there will be so much white on a kitten that it is hard to tell tabby patterns.

Kittens with the most undercoat have the fluffiest appearance and will be the most challenging to groom. Kittens with less undercoat may allow their owners to escape with only weekly thorough grooming, except during the shedding seasons, usually April and August.

A word of warning: Without daily grooming, your Persian may start to resist weekly grooming rituals.

Grooming Tools

Nail clipper: The single most important grooming tool is a nail clipper. Always start by checking the nails to see if they need clipping. Some will find the small human nail clippers work well on young kittens, the larger clippers on adult males. Others will find it most comfortable to invest in a professional "guillotine"-style nail clipper. Experiment until you find one comfortable to use.

Daily Grooming Tools
✔ Long sharp-toothed comb
✔ Nail clippers
✔ Pin brush
✔ Thinning shears

Comb: Now that you have the nails under control, you will want to turn to your next most important grooming tool, the long, sharp-toothed steel comb. Known by various brand names, the Belgian groomer or Greyhound comb is a significant investment, costing around $20. This is the only comb that will reach into the depths of the fine wooly undercoat and prevent the mats before they work their way to the surface of the coat. It is well worth the investment. You may find these on-line or through a local grooming shop. The combs in the supermarket will not fit the bill; they do not have the very long teeth or sharp points needed to reach to the base of the coat, and to stay ahead of the matting.

Coat Care

In addition to the steel comb and nail clippers, a pin brush and thinning shears should be acquired. The brush, while it will not locate or remove mats, will lift the coat and add fluffiness without removing much coat. The thinning shears are to aid in mat removal.

Combing—A Matter of Importance

A Persian cat should, if possible, be combed every day; combing the cat once a week is the absolute minimum. I have seen Persian cats with hair so tangled that it formed hard feltlike layers right next to the skin, so that the veterinarian was forced to anesthetize the animal

and shave it. Especially during shedding season (spring and fall) and often in neutered animals, the undercoat is so fine that it becomes matted in no time. Start grooming your kitten regularly while it is still young, alternating strokes of petting with gentle strokes of the comb. For proper grooming you will need two metal combs, one fine-toothed, the other with the teeth set more widely apart. Start the session with the coarser comb and use it with special thoroughness on the undercoat of the belly and between the legs. Be sure to keep talking softly to the cat and petting it with one hand while the other wields the comb. Never try to use force. Your cat should enjoy being combed. After the first combing, go over the entire coat once more with the fine-tooth comb.

Painless Mat Removal

✔ Never try to remove mats after bathing. You will have a hopeless tangle and a cat at the end of its patience.

✔ Never try to use scissors to remove mats. Like your own child's hair, separate the mat starting at the base of the skin, and with your fingers carefully separate each hair until the mat is free. The cat will become very resistant to grooming if you try to use combs or brushes to accomplish this.

✔ With thick mats, hold the mat away from the skin. Place the thinning shears in the center of the mat, and carefully chomp through the middle of the mat. Then separate the mat in pieces.

✔ If you find regular grooming or shedding beyond your tolerance level, or find yourself too ill, talk to your veterinarian or groomer about the "lion cut." Never shave the tip of the tail; for some reason this seems to trigger the prey instinct, resulting in many cats mutilating the tail tip.

Centuries of careful breeding have resulted in a gentle cat with a sturdy, patient personality. Just as there are throwbacks in type, there are unfortunately occasional throwbacks in personality. Bold kittens may have a shy littermate, or one that is a hellion to be groomed. These kittens should be neutered and placed with understanding owners, preferably ones with a good sense of humor and willing to keep them shaved to a lion cut.

Brushing and Powdering

To keep your cat's coat beautiful and glossy, it should be brushed every day, preferably with a brush of natural bristles. About once a month you can clean the fur with powder, which should, however, be applied sparingly in order not to dry out the skin. Pet supply stores always have some new items of cat cosmetics on display, as do cat shows, of course. There even are special powders for cats with colored fur, but for a cat with light-colored fur, ordinary baby powder is perfectly adequate.

Important: Leave the powder on only overnight, and brush it out carefully the next morning, brushing against the lay of the hair.

Shaving

For really thick wooly coats, the simplest course is to take in the cat for a twice yearly shaving at the grooming shop.

Brush your Persian cat with natural bristles to bring out the full sheen of its coat. Frequent combing and brushing are absolutely essential for Persian cats; it is the only way to keep their fur silky, soft, and lustrous.

The lion cut: A charming shave-down by the local groomer will be an inexpensive solution, and a guaranteed conversation stopper at your home. Looking rather like a poodle cut, the coat is shaved close on the entire body, leaving legs, head, and tail tip with full coat.

Giving Baths— When and How?

You shouldn't bathe your Persian cat unless it is very dirty or if your veterinarian has recommended a bath as treatment for some disorder. Appropriate shampoos that are also effective against pests are available from the veterinarian or at pet supply stores.

The bath should be given in a warm room. Place the cat in a tub with lukewarm water (86° to 96°F [30°–35°C]). Don't frighten the cat by aiming a stream of water directly at it. The head should stay dry. After washing the animal, rinse the soap out thoroughly, and then pat the cat with a prewarmed towel. After that, the fur can dry completely in a warm

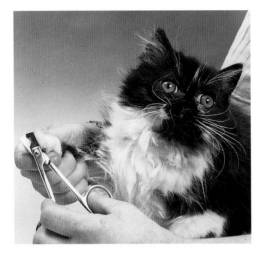

upper left: Keep those claws clipped, and you won't have any worries about your furniture! Notice the cat is not at all distressed.

upper right: A grooming stand that can be raised and lowered is an excellent back-saving investment.

middle: Dab eyes with a cotton ball to help keep stains at bay. And breed for far apart eyes to eliminate crimped tear ducts that cause this problem.

bottom: Eyes begin to open around the age of 10–14 days. Watch for swelling, which indicates an infection, quite common, may be lurking behind the sealed lid.

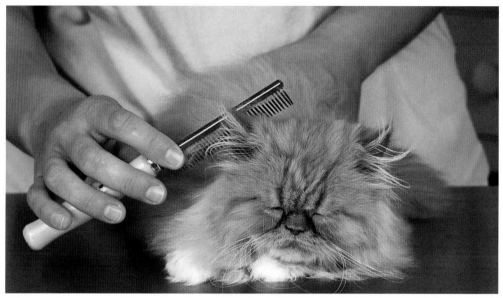

Alternate between combing a favorite spot, such as the ruff or neck, with the least favorite sensitive areas, such as the back legs.

This solid black has superb eye color.

A very pregnant shaded silver. She may begin to look this way after six weeks. Persians tend to deliver later, about 68 days from the first day of breeding.

room. Some Persian cats don't mind being dried with a hair dryer if they have gotten used to it as kittens.

Note: Owners of show cats often bathe their animals before any show to make the coat look as silky and fluffy as possible. For this purpose, color-tint shampoos (matching the color the Persian cat) are especially useful. They are sold by pet supply stores. But regular baby shampoo will also do. Bathe the cat one or two days before the show.

What to Do About Greasy Tails

Unneutered tomcats tend to develop what is called "stud" tail, even though it occasionally occurs also in neutered males or even in females. In a cat with greasy tail, the glands on the upper side of the tail, and especially at the root of the tail, secrete too much fat, making the tail look greasy and yellowish brown. In long-haired Persian cats, this looks particularly bad because all the tail hairs become greasy. You can wash the tail with baby shampoo, letting the shampoo soak in well in the greasy spots and then scrubbing them gently with a soft toothbrush. Do this several times, until the tail is clean. It is better, of course, to prevent greasy tail from developing. To do this, you can rub some talcum powder into the hair on the tail once or twice a week. Leave the powder on overnight, then brush it all out the next day.

Using a surgical scrub (consult your veterinarian) several days in a row also helps.

Note: Comb and brush the tail very gently; tail hairs that are pulled out take a long time to grow back in.

Care of the Toenails

Persian cats have sharp claws but are often too lazy to use them enough. It is therefore a good idea to trim the nails of the front paws once or twice a month with special nail clippers (available at pet supply stores). Cut off only the tips of the claws, where there are no blood vessels. Watch your veterinarian do this a few times before attempting it yourself.

Note: If you plan to show your Persian cat at an exhibition, it is particularly considerate toward the judge to trim your cat's claws the day before.

Proper Care of Eyes and Ears

Eyes: Persian cats that have a pronounced *stop* as prescribed by the breed standard (see page 7) may have tear ducts that are narrow or even blocked. Conscientious breeders are working to eliminate tearing by breeding for eyes that are very far apart, thus getting rid of the crimping of the tear ducts as well as the resulting excessive tearing. Teary eyes leave ugly yellowish brown spots on the fur. You

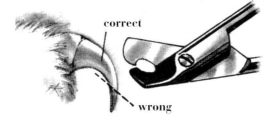

correct

wrong

To trim the claws, hold each toe steady between your fingers, one at a time. Then nip off the tip of the claw well below the blood vessels with special nail clippers.

Grooming Routines

Daily	Weekly	Monthly	Less Than Monthly
Combing	Check/clip nails	Check ears for dark exudates	April: lion cut
Brushing	Bathe face	Check penis for hair lodged in sheath	August: second lion cut
Tooth brushing	Closely check eyes for injuries		
Clean eyes		Trim bottom fur around tail and "pantaloons"	
	Check for chin acne		

should therefore wipe away the discharge from the eyes several times a day with a paper tissue. Always wipe in the direction away from the ears and toward the nose. The veterinarian can also give you eyedrops that reduce the tearing.

Ears: The ears should be checked regularly. Clean dirty ears carefully with a cotton swab moistened with lukewarm water. Never dig around in the ear; confine your efforts to the external ear.

Checking Teeth and Gums

Even cats that are fed a nutritionally excellent diet don't always have perfect teeth. Cats unfortunately tend to develop gingivitis (inflammation of the gums) and buildup of tartar. That is why it is important to regularly check the mouth of your Persian cat. Once yearly veterinary dental cleaning will help, as will daily tooth brushing.

Show Grooming

The languid beauty on the judging stand plays lazily with the pheasant feather, oblivious to the chaos of the surrounding crowds. But will you be able to find a kitten like this one? Over 100 generations of breeding have gone into producing this show personality, carefully bred to accept the daily grooming with calm acceptance.

The disposition of the Persian is set first in heredity and nurtured for an amenable teddy bear temperament. Persians must be willing to be laid on their backs, resisting the natural urge to protect their vital parts in a daily grooming ritual. From birth they are handled and trained to regard this grooming as part of their daily life.

Those kittens that do not meet the show standard will be placed in pet homes, but should come from a home where early training will make daily grooming a pleasure rather than a chore.

When ill, your Persian is likely to greet you at the door, cry softly, lead you to its favorite sleeping area, and then lie down. Looking up at you with a another cry, it can hardly say any more clearly, "Mom, I hurt!" More often, the owner will find that the cat does not greet them at the door, but has taken refuge in a closet or is simply curled up in the corner, suffering in silence.

Ailments

Any change in the normal greeting behavior is a serious sign of illness and should not be taken lightly. A major cause of this sudden behavior shift is an extremely dangerous and immediately life-threatening urinary tract problem. Call the veterinarian immediately and rush the cat to him or her. With a urinary tract blockage, hours are critical in successful treatment. If blocked, a cat may be fine in the morning and near death from uremia by evening. If in kidney failure, the disease may take days, months, or years to run its course.

The Persian is a sturdy cat and can withstand many ailments. With its heavy weight, it is a

Cameo Persian, free of eye stains, and with an even full coat and chubby muzzle. The picture of health. Like the silver Persian, the tipped pattern gene is expressed in both deeper and shallow tipping, creating both shaded and chinchilla, both with red tipping and copper eyes, rather than black tipping and green eyes.

champ at living off its fat when an upper respiratory ailment or a case of diarrhea strikes. The owner will find that his/her Persians will survive poisonings and infections that often leave less sturdy cats with far less fat stores dead.

However, like all cats they are subject to a variety of inherited diseases that know no boundaries, except that of the conscientious breeder who maintains tested animals, and breeds out the affected cats. Following is a list of major known defects of cats. It might be noted that these have been identified in all breeds, and a cat from the animal shelter is equally at risk of these diseases.

Congenital Diseases

Genetic defects occur quite readily in free-ranging cats. But as scientists are lacking knowledge of the breeding history of the parents or grandparents, it is very hard to determine if the defect occurred through damage in the womb or if the defect was inherited. Cats from shelters are most often neutered, so scientists seldom have the ability to establish a breeding population of the defect.

Some Persian breeders keep remarkably detailed pedigrees and breeding records on their cats, and that, in fact, seems to be one of the great joys of breeding cats. There are even on-line Linechaser groups, which spend hours chasing down pedigree bloodlines, poring over old catalogs and stacks of pedigrees. These groups maintain not only breeding records, on-line, but sometimes are on the front lines of identifying genetic defects.

Polycystic Kidney Disease

In the late 1990s, reports began in Europe of uncommon kidney diseases occurring in Persians imported from the United States. In Sweden, ultrasound testing was done, and the culprit identified as an inherited kidney disease, with more than 90 percent of the imported Persian lines being affected.

Also occurring in millions of humans throughout the world, the disorder results in the erosion of the kidneys. Huge cysts are formed, progressing until the kidneys resemble Swiss cheese. The cat may die in infancy—in humans more than 60 percent die at a young age—or live to adulthood, passing the disorders on to its offspring. A dominant gene means that cats with PKD can be neutered and the gene can be more readily eliminated from the gene pool.

Low-cost clinics have rapidly spread across the country, where veterinary specialists with very sensitive ultrasound machines are willing to test cats for very low rates, usually less than $40 per cat. These clinics tested more than 10,000 Persians before statistics stopped being compiled at the web site. More than 39 percent of the Persians tested had the disease,

seemingly healthy breeding adult animals and their older kittens. Not included were young kittens, since the ultrasound may miss early cysts when the kittens are under the age of six months and in those that were stillborn.

Recent clinics at the University of California, Davis have been free, since Dr. Leslie Lyons, a visiting scientist there, has been collecting mouth swab samples to see if a DNA marker can identify the disease in healthy cats. At present, only very high-resolution ultrasounds with experienced operators are adept at identifying the disease.

A breeder may take in ten cats to these clinics, and find that four, five, or even all the cats have the disease. They must then determine and balance the need to continue the bloodlines against the need to alter all affected cats. Some will choose to save an affected breeding male, then test and clear his offspring. The obvious disadvantage, since this is a dominant gene and may be passed to 50 percent of kittens, is that these must either be kept or placed with very understanding owners. These affected kittens are much like children with the disease—some will die in infancy, some before the age of two or three years, and others may live much longer. The author has a PKD-affected grand champion that is still alive at age 13. All of her affected offspring have died before the age of eight.

Treatment: The only method known at present of treating the disease is kidney transplantation, a very expensive procedure undertaken at a few veterinary clinics and teaching hospitals across the United States. However, in the search for pharmaceutical treatment of the disease in humans, very promising results have been found in some ACTH compounds that will slow the formation of the cysts and subsequent damage to the kidney—not a cure, but a hope of a stopgap measure.

Progressive Retinal Atrophy

An adult cat becoming gradually blind is the first symptom noticed by the veterinarian. Caused by a recessive gene that affects the retinal structures at the back of the eye, the vision is gradually destroyed through damage to the retina's light-receiving rods and cones. While this disease has been followed in the Abyssinian breed for many years, it has only recently been discovered in the gene pool of Persians as well. Frequently passed off as an upper respiratory infection, the disease is not apparent in young animals, requiring maturity for the identifiable symptoms to appear. An examination by a certified veterinary ophthalmologist will help identify those affected animals early. Until a DNA marker is identified for this disease, testing offspring is the only way of identifying affected cats. The veterinarians are not able to identify carriers, except by the logic of hindsight. That is, a blind offspring had to have both parents carrying the defective gene.

Once again, the breeder must make hard choices, in this case even more difficult, because it is a recessive gene. This means a cat can carry the gene without ever developing the symptoms, yet passing the gene along to 50 percent of its offspring. When two unaffected cats, each carrying the recessive gene, are bred together, one quarter of their offspring will be affected. Given a cat's penchant for keeping its owners from rearranging the household, a cat gradually becoming blind as an adult may live its entire life without its owners being fully aware of the problem.

Infections

While infections may be influenced by the physical condition, the most important elements in battling infections are an inherited resistance of the cat and the cat's treatment in the home environment. A cold basement or garage at night, dirty water bowls, and infrequent litter pan changes are all contributors to a poor environment for a cat's health. Think of what your own health would be like if you were forced to deal with these home conditions.

When scientists try to identify those animals that are high on the list to be used as test subjects, and to be kept in colonies, cats are listed as very difficult, due to their susceptibility to upper respiratory infection. These are very hard to clear, since like the human cold, the virus readily mutates. Regular vaccinations do help prevent the spread of these and other infectious diseases however.

A Healthy Cat vs. a Sick Cat

If your Persian cat shows a lively interest in the world around it, behaves normally, looks well fed, has a thick, glossy coat and clear, bright eyes, and licks itself enough to stay absolutely clean, you can generally assume that it is healthy.

If you observe the behavior of your Persian cat attentively every day when you comb it, you will notice quickly if anything is wrong. When you feed the cat, you see how much it has eaten, and when you clean out the litter box you can examine its excrements carefully.

Signs of illness: Lack of appetite, rapid weight loss, sudden changes in behavior, apathy, neglect of cleanliness, dull fur, hair falling out, itching, frequent attempts to urinate and defecate, bloating of the body, constant vomiting, increased thirst, diarrhea.

If you notice any of these changes, you should immediately take the cat to the veterinarian.

Preventive Health Care

You can protect your Persian from some medical problems by taking preventive measures.

Worming

Cats often have roundworms. Adult cats get infected with worm eggs they pick up on the ground or lick off their fur, and kittens absorb them through their mother's milk. Tapeworms are not so common in Persian cats because these cats generally live indoors and have little contact with mice, which are the carriers of this parasite. Worms lessen the organism's resistance to infectious diseases and can interfere with the effectiveness of immunization. That is why you should have your Persian cat checked regularly for worms and have it wormed several times a year.

Dangerous Infectious Diseases

There are a number of infectious diseases that may endanger your Persian cat's life and against which only regular vaccination offers protection.

Distemper (Feline Panleucopenia)

Possible symptoms: Vomiting, diarrhea, pain (manifested by cries when the cat's body is touched), apathy, fever, dehydration.

Treatment: Treatment generally offers no hope; however, immunization prevents infection.

Respiratory Diseases

The term "cat flu" is used for several different kinds of respiratory disease affecting the mucous membranes of the sinuses, the nose, and other respiratory passages. Most common of these are calcivirus and rhinotrachitis.

Possible symptoms: Discharge from the eyes that may be clear or yellow with pus, plugged nostrils; often accompanied by sneezing and breathing difficulties. Frequently, though not always, the affected animal is apathetic.

Treatment: Take the cat to the veterinarian immediately! Sometimes, cats recover from an infection quite well because there are relatively harmless forms of it, but in many cases it proves fatal. There is a vaccine against the most dangerous viruses (rhinotrachitis and calcivirus) responsible for cat flu.

Rabies

Rabies is a viral disease that has to be reported to health officials. It is transmitted to other animals and to humans through the bite of an infected animal.

Symptoms: Abnormal behavior, salivating, paralysis.

Treatment: There is no cure for rabies; it is always fatal. Persian cats that are let out occasionally should definitely get a yearly rabies shot. For cats that are shown at exhibitions or that travel abroad, rabies shots are mandatory.

Feline Leukemia

Possible symptoms: Leukemia often goes undetected because it can take different forms. Some signs are emaciation, lack of immunal defenses, swelling of the lymph nodes, anemia.

Treatment: Leukemia is incurable and highly contagious. Infected animals must be kept

Normal Physical Signs of Adult Cats

Temperature:	100° to 102.5°F (37.8°–39.2°C)
Breathing:	20 to 40 breaths per minute
Pulse rate:	100 to 140 beats per minute
Appearance of feces:	Moist and soft, dark gray to brown, well shaped
Appearance of urine:	Clear and yellow; the urine of a sexually mature male cat has an unpleasant smell.

separate from healthy ones. There is a test that shows whether or not a cat has leukemia, and there is also an effective vaccine against this deadly disease.

Aujeszky's Disease

Possible symptoms: Abnormal behavior. Itching is a characteristic symptom, but it doesn't occur in all cases.

Treatment: As of now there is no treatment for this disease, which always ends in death. To prevent infection, you should keep your cat from eating raw or partially cooked pork or beef or raw butcher's scraps.

FIV (Feline Immune Deficiency Virus, previously known as Feline T-lymphotropic Lenti Virus)

It became apparent in 1987 that a virus is prevalent in cats that resembles the AIDS virus in humans. This virus can cause disease symptoms in cats, but the symptoms don't necessarily lead to death.

Possible symptoms: The symptoms are so vague and unspecific that the disease is difficult to diagnose, but since early 1989 a simple test to determine the presence of this virus has been available to veterinarians.

Treatment: There is at this point no way to cure this disease. It is contagious, but only to other felines.

Feline Infectious Peritonitis

Symptoms: Typically, this disease manifests itself in a bloated body caused by retention of fluid in the abdominal and pectoral cavities; also, lack of appetite, emaciation, lethargy, fever, tumors. But there are also atypical cases in which death comes quickly without any of these characteristic signs.

Treatment: Take the cat to the veterinarian immediately even though there is, at this point, no treatment that offers hope of cure. It is contagious among cats.

Less Serious Ailments

While not inherited and certainly not infectious, these ailments left untreated may lead to life-threatening situations.

Vomiting

Symptoms: Throwing up of food with violent retching movements, contraction of the abdominal muscles, and coughlike noises.

Possible causes: Cats vomit very easily by nature. They even eat grass and other plants to make themselves throw up. Persian cats frequently get rid of hair they have swallowed in the course of grooming themselves by coughing up hair balls. The retching movements and noises are often mistaken for coughing. If a cat keeps vomiting for some time, and if it throws up after every meal, this indicates a serious illness.

Treatment: In case of prolonged vomiting, call the veterinarian.

Constipation

Symptoms: A constipated cat goes to its box and tries, often many times in the course of a day, to pass stool by straining painfully. If constipation persists, the belly becomes swollen and the cat loses its appetite.

Possible causes: Older Persian cats are particularly prone to constipation. Lack of exercise seems to contribute to the problem. Often, hair balls plug up the intestines, which causes constipation.

Treatment: With many cats, feeding them milk, or a teaspoonful of mineral oil daily for a few days, counteracts constipation. Gentle massaging of the abdomen and an enema can also help. To prevent problems with hair balls, you should give your Persian cat a little butter or margarine from time to time. If constipation is not relieved within 24 hours or if it recurs, you should take the animal to the veterinarian. Frequent dosing with mineral oil may affect the absorption of various vitamins, and a multivitamin supplement should be given to compensate.

Diarrhea

Symptoms: Runny feces, dirty fur in the area around the anus.

Possible causes: Intestinal problems, especially in kittens. If the cat is otherwise cheerful and behaves normally, there is no immediate cause for worry.

Treatment: Food should be withheld immediately. Make sure the cat drinks enough to prevent dehydration. After a day of fasting, the cat may be given small amounts of cooked meat or liver and some dry or canned cat food. When the consistency of the feces is normal again, you can resume usual feedings—but give no milk or raw liver. If the diarrhea resumes, you have to consult the veterinarian.

Parasites

Parasites may be internal, such as worms, or external, such as fungus or insects. Some are shared equally among all warm-blooded members of the household (cats, dogs, humans, and, occasionally, birds). Others are species specific, such as the cat roundworm, and cannot infect dogs, humans, or birds. Cat mites, cat fleas, and cat lice cannot thrive on humans, but can cause allergic skin responses, not to mention the sensation of creepy crawlies on the skin.

Fleas

Symptoms: Scratching, skin changes, weight loss, pale mucous membranes, changes in behavior.

Possible source: Contact with infested animals. Although there are special cat fleas, cats can also become infested with dog fleas or other kinds.

Treatment: There are very effective flea applications available from your veterinarian or at pet shops. It is important to clean and vacuum well, especially in the places where your cat likes to sleep, to get rid of flea eggs and larvae.

Lice

Symptoms: Cat lice are tiny (about $\frac{1}{20}$ of an inch [1.3 mm] long), yellowish, and can be seen crawling around in the fur with the naked eye. Cat lice are not transmitted to humans.

Possible source: Contact with lice-infested animals.

Treatment: The same products you use against fleas are effective against lice.

Ticks

Symptoms: Ticks attach themselves to the head of a cat or other parts of the body. They are pea-sized, shiny, and gray. Paralysis may result.

Possible source: Cats get ticks outdoors. Ticks drop from trees and bushes onto animals or people that pass by and then dig their mouthparts into the skin to suck blood.

Treatment: Ticks can be daubed with oil, then grasped with tweezers, and removed by turning them like a screw.

Important note: The increase in reported cases of tick-borne ailments (Lyme disease, for example) is most likely due to the increasing population of host animals (raccoons, deer, and opossum) moving into areas in which they have been scarce before. The ticks will then leave the animal it has infected and will seek a new host such as a cat or a human.

Humans cannot "catch" a tick-borne disease from a cat; however, they can become infected by the same tick that is transmitting the disease. It is impossible to eradicate ticks from all areas, but try to keep your cat away from known tick-infested areas such as open fields. It is also a good practice to inspect your cat for ticks each time it returns to the house. Be sure to check inside the ears and between the toes.

Ringworm

Symptoms: Hair breaks off and falls out (often causing round bald spots); sometimes accompanied by itching.

Cause: This condition is caused by a skin fungus that can be transmitted to humans.

Treatment: If you suspect a fungus infection, have the veterinarian check the cat. Combating this condition is complicated. Internal and external treatments and strict disinfecting measures have to be continued over a long period of time. Studies show lime sulfur dips combined with shaving is the most effective treatment.

Mites

Symptoms: Itching, frequent shaking of the head, mangy areas; in serious cases, tilting of the head and upset equilibrium.

Possible source: Contact with infested animals. Cats are subject to attack from different kinds of mites (the cause of mange). Ear mites are relatively common, often causing serious inflammation of the auditory canal.

Treatment: If you suspect mites, take your cat to the veterinarian immediately!

Toxoplasmosis

Possible symptoms: This disease usually produces no symptoms, but lack of appetite as well as constipation or diarrhea can be signs.

Cause: Toxoplasmosis is caused by a protozoan (*Toxoplasma gondii*) that multiplies within the cells of higher organisms. Humans, too, can be infected with this pathogen, but the human body produces antibodies that suppress the infection. However, toxoplasmosis poses a serious risk to the unborn babies of women who are exposed to the pathogen for

Health Check

Part of Body	How It Should Look	How It Should Not Look
Anus	Clean, without trace of feces	Bits of excreta smeared around it
Breathing	Quiet, even	Panting, abrupt
Eyes	Clear, bright, wide open	Teary; with sticky secretion; exposed third eyelid
Coat	Glossy, clean	Dull, greasy, sticking out from body; parasite infested
Skin	Dry, smooth	Scaly or greasy; with round, red spots or eczema
Lymph nodes	Normal to the touch	Swollen
Nose	Dry and cool	Wet; with whitish or yellowish discharge
Ears	Absolutely clean	Black, sticky secretion (possible sign of mites); red (inflammation)
Pulse	Steady	Too fast or too slow (for normal pulse rate)
Teeth	Whitish, without deposit	Brownish gray, with tartar deposits
Gums	A healthy pink	Either too pale or bright red; bad breath

the first time during pregnancy. That is why attention to hygiene in handling cats is especially important during pregnancy. Toxoplasmosis is most often caused by the consumption of raw meat (in the case of humans, usually pork). If a cat is never given raw meat to eat and has no contact with the feces of other cats, it will not get infected.

Physical Injuries

Symptoms: Limping, staggering, hiding, bleeding wounds, lack of appetite, breathing difficulties, apathy.

Possible causes: Because most Persian cats are kept indoors, the danger of accidental injuries is small. But they often get hurt getting trapped in a casement window when trying to escape outdoors. If the cat is not freed promptly, it may suffocate or die of spinal injuries. Falling from a great height, as from a window or balcony, is also very dangerous.

Treatment: If a cat has sustained wounds or if you suspect internal injuries or fractures, help from a veterinarian is necessary. Light external injuries that don't affect the cat's general state significantly usually heal quickly without any special treatment.

Vaccination Schedule

	Distemper	Respiratory Diseases	Rabies	Leukemia
First vaccination possible at:	8 weeks	8 weeks	8 weeks	8 weeks
Booster shot for cats under 12 weeks old	after 3–4 weeks	after 2–4 weeks	after 3–4 weeks	first after 3–4 weeks second after 2–4 months third after 1 year
Booster shot for cats 12 weeks old or older	after 1 year	after 2–4 weeks	after 1 year	first after 3–4 weeks second after 2–4 months third after 1 year
Regular vaccinations to keep up immunization	every 2 years	annual	annual	annual

Poisoning

Symptoms: Lack of appetite, breathing difficulties, tearing eyes, diarrhea, repeated vomiting, weight loss, exposed third eyelid, pallor of the mucous membranes, constipation, abnormal behavior.

Possible causes: The most common poisonous substances a Persian cat kept indoors is likely to come into contact with are mineral oil, herbicides, and mouse or rat poisons (see List of Dangers table, page 42). Cats have a natural aversion to spoiled food; also, their gastric juices usually kill any pathogens found in such food. Some of the severe infectious diseases can lead to death so quickly that the owner is often convinced that the cat was poisoned. However, poisoning is rather rare in cats.

Treatment: If you suspect poisoning, take the cat to the veterinarian immediately.

Conjunctivitis

Symptoms: Inflammation of eye's outer membranes, formation of pus, and swelling of the eyelids. This condition also occurs in newborn kittens whose eyes are not yet open. There is often an accumulation of pus underneath the closed lids.

Causes: The disease agents are usually chlamydia and mycoplasma. In kittens, the inflammation is generally caused by bacteria that attack the mucous membranes.

Treatment: Most cases of conjunctivitis respond well to treatment with ophthalmic antibiotic ointment, sometimes combined with a drug to reduce soreness. Others, however, require lengthy treatment by the veterinarian as well as general good care and a nutritious diet.

Important note: If the condition is neglected in newborn kittens, it can lead to blindness.

Eye Ulcers and Corneal Sequestra

Symptoms: Squinting. Close examination may reveal scooped out areas on the surface of the eye, or dark spots in the iris.

Causes: Injury, respiratory viruses, possibly hereditary tendency.

Treatment: See a veterinarian immediately. Quick treatment with ointment or surgery may save the eye.

Infections of the Respiratory System

Symptoms: Breathing difficulties, coughing, lack of appetite, swollen lymph nodes, exposed third eyelids, salivating, abnormal behavior. Inherent in all infections of the respiratory system is the danger of pneumonia, which brings on high fever and apathy and can lead to death.

Possible causes: Viruses, bacteria, fungi.

Treatment: Visit the veterinarian immediately!

Important note: Because of their short nose and the stop, which the standard calls for, Persian cats may breathe very noisily even when there is no infection of the respiratory passages.

Urinary Tract and Sexual Organ Diseases

Immensely dangerous, subtle in symptoms, these diseases readily kill cats without veterinary intervention. These constitute major medical emergencies.

Infection of the Uterus (Pyometra)

Symptoms; Increased thirst, swollen abdomen, lack of appetite, and frequently, but not always, a pink or brownish vaginal discharge that the cat often licks off. Later the cat becomes apathetic and the fur turns dull.

Causes: This condition may be caused by pathogens or by a hormonal imbalance. It is more common in cats that have been treated with hormones or cats that have been in heat for a long time, suffering perhaps from permanent heat, and have not mated at all or have not conceived.

Treatment: If the cat is not to be used for breeding, removal of the uterus and the ovaries is usually the best solution. Trying to cure the infection generally involves lengthy prostaglandin treatment and makes sense only in the case of very valuable breeding animals. One way to prevent the problem from arising is to spay the cat (see page 61).

Bladder Stones

Symptoms: The cat keeps going to its litter box and tries to urinate, often while emitting cries of pain. There may be blood in the urine.

Possible causes: Wrong diet, hereditary factors, possibly pathogens. If the urinary tract gets blocked, the cat quickly (within hours) dies of uremia.

Treatment: A thorough examination by the veterinarian is always necessary if symptoms of this condition are observed.

Dental Problems

Daily toothbrushing? Absolutely. Your pet store has some tasty (to cats) toothpastes. Dental preventatives, such as yearly teeth cleaning to remove stubborn tarter, can extend the life of your cat by 10 or more years.

Tartar

Symptoms: The teeth, especially in the back of the mouth, are covered with a grayish white to brownish deposit.

Possible cause: In some cat families there seems to be a hereditary tendency for tartar formation.

Treatment: The veterinarian can remove the tartar by means of an ultrasonic dental scaler under anesthesia. Daily toothbrushing helps.

Gingivitis

Symptoms: Often a buildup of tartar (a grayish white to brownish deposit on the teeth) is accompanied by bad breath and persistent inflammation of the gums (gingivitis). The gums are dark red and bleed easily.

Possible causes: Hereditary tendency, but sometimes some internal infection.

Treatment: Take the cat to the veterinarian immediately!

Visits to the Veterinarian

Take your Persian cat in a sturdy and securely locked carrier, for there are bound to be other animals in the waiting room.

Important information: The veterinarian will need a history and symptoms of the condition, as well as your observation on how the cat has been eating, appearance and frequency of excretions, and changes in behavior, if any.

Note: Never try to treat a sick cat yourself without veterinary advice.

Nursing a Sick Cat

Physical and psychological care: A very sick cat or one that has undergone surgery should be placed in a clean cardboard box in a warm, quiet, and familiar spot at home. Make a pad of several layers of newspapers covered with a clean flannel sheet for the cat to lie on. If the cat is too sick to lick itself, it should be cleaned with a damp cloth after it has eaten and defecated.

Feeding: If the cat is unable to eat on its own for some time, you should, after consulting with your veterinarian, force-feed it beef paste or other highly concentrated high-energy foods that come in paste form. Even more important than food is a constant supply of liquids. Homemade beef or chicken broth, without any seasoning, can be given with a plastic syringe.

Giving medicines: As long as a cat can eat, medicines can be concealed in small chunks of meat or other favorite tidbits. If you have to make a cat swallow pills, capsules, or tablets, tilt its head up slightly, force open the mouth, push the medicine as far down into the throat as you can, and then hold the cat's mouth shut with your hand. Massage the throat with the fingers of your free hand to make the cat swallow. Medicines in liquid form are given with a plastic syringe that is inserted between the cheek and the back teeth while you hold up the cat's head slightly. Sometimes cats refuse to swallow a medicine but readily lick it off their paws.

Low body temperature: Don't force-feed a cat or kitten with a low body temperature. The enzymes that digest the food are not active at low temperatures, causing the food to sit in the stomach and spoil. Kittens with low body temperature should be given nourishment with an IV or with periotoneal fluids by your veterinarian.

CAT SHOWS

The day is hot, the nose may be offended by the odor, the ears struck by the quiet hush of the hall. And throughout the large building elaborately decorated cages greet the public. Suddenly the words "Cat out!" ring through the hall. Doors slam shut, the exhibitors all freeze in place, the public continues to mill about, not sure of what is happening. The cat's afoot!

The Excitement of the Show

Stand quite still, because somewhere, some-one is crawling under the tables and through the paraphernalia stored there, trying to find and recapture their panicked cat. Once found, a carrier will be brought and the kitty escorted back to its cage or, if it didn't already escape by biting the judge, into the judging ring.

There is more than one judge in the hall, usually six or eight judges. Each will eventually, over a two-day period, handle, judge, and place every single cat in the hall. It is an exhausting prospect for the exhibitors, the judges, and the cats. But there is an excitement in the air as well, a feeling of anticipation and expectations not quite realized. Some people are gathered, by invitation only, around buffets or at their home cages, others are chatting in groups, while nervously watching the judges' rings for their cats' numbers, and yet another is talking to a woman with two children in tow, looking for their first Persian kitten.

A copper-eyed white kitten.

Suddenly the announcement comes: "Prepare your Persian kittens, people!" It is time for one of those eight judges to begin calling up all the Persian kittens in the show hall. Ten by ten, from the lowest assigned catalog numbers, which are the white Persian kittens, to the very last kitten, which will be the Himalayan color classes, the kittens arrive for judging.

Calls ring out again: "Third and final call for Kitten number 19!" Clearly the person has been stopped while bringing the kitten to the ring, or was in the middle of the buffet at the other end of the show hall, or selling a kitten, and will come rushing up to deliver the kitten to a now irritated judge.

Finding Shows

These days the best place to locate shows is to go to each association's web site and look for the show schedule. A hall has to have at least 14,000 square feet, which rules out many small towns, unless they have a county fair-ground with a large single building available.

As a result, most shows are held in larger cities, and mostly on weekends.

Judging

The judging hours will usually be from about 10:00 A.M. to 4:00 P.M. If there are eight judges, likely the show will be two days long. This is what the dog show people call a "bench show." Cats do not go to and from the hall during the day, unless pulled from the ring for illness or other family emergencies. The cats and their owners are expected to stay in the hall that entire time, leaving about 4:00 P.M. each day to rest the cats for the next day's judging.

Each judge will separately judge the kittens, the adults, and the altered (neutered) cats, as well as any household pets categories. The judge picks out the ten Best Kittens, ten Best Adults, ten Best Alters, so a kitten might have eight rosettes on its cage, one from each judging! There is seldom a Best of the Best judging held on the second day, the equivalent of the Best in Show in dog shows. Each ring instead is considered its own separate show, with its own Best in Show.

Where Are the Persians?

At most shows the cats are placed randomly in the benching areas, and friends often ask to be "benched" with each other, so you might find eight silver Persian exhibitors in one spot, and another few scattered throughout the hall. Some will have signs on their cages with cards advertising kittens at home for sale; a few may even have a kitten for sale at the show—especially if they live in a county that forbids the breeding and sale of kittens in homes, a recent

Junior Showmanship

Some shows have established special categories for young exhibitors to encourage the proper care of cats and also the next generation of exhibitors. This early training in exhibiting cats may provide families with the opportunity to participate more fully in the cat show experience. The classes are held by the judges and involve the child in handling their own cat before the public.

development by some groups to prevent the breeding of purebred kittens.

Cat Associations

Cat associations are made up of and represent the interests of keepers, breeders, and lovers of all kinds of cats. Their aims are to encourage the production of purebred pedigreed cats and to promote optimal living conditions for cats kept as pets. The clubs try to realize their goals by bringing together breeders and fanciers of different breeds of cats, by facilitating the exchange of breeding experiences at meetings, in specialized publications, and by organizing scientific lectures. Through these means, they make available theoretical and practical knowledge on all aspects of keeping cats: breeding, genetics, grooming, nutrition, principles of judging at shows, and how to find cats and kittens of breeding quality.

The Actual Shows

Cats were exhibited as early as the sixteenth century, but the first exhibition that is comparable to our modern cat shows was held in London in 1871.

International exhibitions usually last for two days and are always held on weekends. Depending on the size of the hall, between 200 and 1,000 cats are shown.

Going to a cat show is especially useful for giving you an overall impression of what is expected in a cat of a certain breed. The judges evaluate cats by comparing them to their breed standard.

Which Cats Can Be Entered in a Show?

Any Persian cat that is healthy, clean, and vaccinated may be entered in a show. Even an ordinary, unpedigreed household pet may compete in the so-called Household Pet or Non-Pedigreed section.

Preparations in the Exhibition Hall

On the first day, usually a Saturday, the cats are "checked in" between 7:00 and 9:00 A.M. Application forms and vaccination records have to be shown at the door, pen or cage numbers are assigned, and the animals may be briefly examined by a veterinarian. Then the cat's pen must be found, disinfected, and decorated. Bring along curtains that fit a pen 28 × 28 × 28 inches (70 × 70 × 70 cm) and hang them inside from sets of stretched wire sold for use with windows of recreational vehicles. Also have a soft pad for the cat to lie on and a litter box in the pen. Then the cat gets its final brushing and is placed in its pen. Persian cats are usually ideal exhibition objects because they spend most of their time sleeping.

Show Classes and Winners' Titles

When you fill out the official registration form, you have to enter your cat in one of three show classes: Non-Championship, Championship, and Premiership. (Non-Championship classes: 1. the *Kitten Class*; 2. the Any Other Variety Class (*AOV Class*); 3. the *Provisional Breed Class*; 4. the *Miscellaneous* (Non-Competitive) *Class*; and 5. the *Household Pet Class*. Championship classes: 1. the *Open Class*; 2. the *Champion Class;* and 3. the *Grand Champion Class.* Premiership classes: 1. Premiership classes for CFA-registered neutered or spayed cats, eight months old or over, that would, as whole cats, be eligible to compete in the Championship classes; and 2. the following classes, recognized only for neuters and spays of each Championship Color Class: Grand Premier, Premier, and Open. The eligibility for each class will be determined in the same manner as for the corresponding class in Championship competition. Wins made in Championship competition may not be transferred to Premiership records. However, titles won in Championship competition are retained. Make very sure that you are entering your cat for the right class; if your cat receives a rating in a class that was not right for it the rating is invalid. Each class is subdivided into the various colors of Persian cats and into male and female. Thus, male Red Persians compete only against other male Red Persians and male Black Persians only against other male Black Persians; the same system applies to females. These winners then compete for Best of Color and Second Best of Color.

Best of Breed

From among all the classes, including the junior classes and neutered cats or spays, the most beautiful representative of the breed is picked. The chosen cat is called "Best of Breed."

BIRTH AND DEATH

Persians are notoriously fickle when it comes to breeding. They may be wildly attached to you, or their neutered playmate, or the neighborhood stray calling back from the fence. They do not travel well to new territories and will often fall from season when taken into strange territory. They are also typically long-lived.

Facts About Breeding

Territory plays a major role in acceptance of stud service by the female. This is definitely not like dog breeding. Dogs' socialization is based on accepted pack behavior. Cat socialization is built on a lion pride structure. As a result, strange males are not readily accepted, and are a threat to any young belonging to the resident male and female.

But where to find a male with which to breed? Call back the breeder of your female; he might be willing to take on one of his own lines, simply to continue to expand his own cat's bloodlines. You may have to take a female to the male's household and leave them there together for one or two seasons before she will accept the male. Even then, she will often attack the male.

Once the female is experienced, she will be much less reluctant to mate with a strange

Even young silvers begin with gray eyes that will clear to brilliant green, while the blue kitten above will clear to khaki, then to copper eyes.

male. If your cat's breeder is no longer in the picture, once again, call CFA Central Office to locate breeders in your area. For the reasons mentioned above, you will likely find few breeders willing to take on a novice female cat.

Females' Season and Males' Urge

By the age of five months, both females and males may begin to sexually mature. They may be old enough to become pregnant or impregnate at five months, but, like a precocious teenager, their bodies and minds may not be yet suited for adult behaviors. Delay breeding females until at least ten months of age. Persian males, on the other hand, are notoriously late bloomers, some not breeding until two years or older. As part of this late maturing process, or through an inherited defect, some male Persians may also retain one or both testes until close to the age of one year, unlike most breeds of cats that drop the testes during the first three months of life.

Females' Season

How will you know your girl is coming into season? Generally, Persians follow the light cycle. As the days grow longer in December, they will begin to rise to their first season. They will sometimes exhibit symptoms of season only late at night, when the household is otherwise quiet and asleep, cooing and calling with a full cry, very unlike their usual squeaky voice. By about the third day of the heat cycle, she will be seducing your ankles, your shoes, the table legs, by rubbing her head against any immovable object. Finally, she begins to put her head to the ground, and dance with her back feet, treading the carpet in a seductive rumba. She will likely stop eating during this period.

Generally, breeding females begin to develop reproductive problems around the age of six, and are altered, while males never seem to lose the urge, but eventually seem to lose the ability around the age of 15. An on-line survey and a study of studbooks shows that females may occasionally breed until the age of 12, males until about 15, though there are records of some breeding into their early 20s. Clearly, altered cats, not subject to the stress of breeding, may live even longer, although the oldest cat known, is a mature stud male Rex-Sphinx cross that lived beyond the age of 30.

If not bred, the cat may stay in season for weeks, resulting in dangerous anorexia. Or she may drop from heat, only to begin cycling again in three weeks. This will continue until after midsummer, when the light cycle begins to shorten the days. By September, she may no longer cycle, but by then your neighbors and members of your household will likely be in full revolt. Worse yet, she may even take to spraying your bed and furniture, marking her territory and advertising her availability.

Males' Urge

If you have a male Persian, reconsider the urge to put him to stud. Male Persians mature a bit later sometimes than the shorthaired males. They will begin signaling their maturity by backing up to drapes, spraying a slight amount of very stinky urine, then repeating on the kitchen cabinets, your sofa, your shoes. Usually, the male is then confined to the porch or the garage, giving lonely piercing cries.

Generally, the odor generated by spraying or the constant mournful crying when the male is locked out of his happy home is not worth the effort. You must have an adequate number of girls to keep him happy and adequate airy quarters for both males and females. He must wear stud pants when in the main part of the house. Your neighbors may have to endure the howling at night and the scent resembling skunk lurking in the air on warm days. If you do not want to deal with the breeding cycle, then American veterinarians are willing to alter kittens as early as three months, assuming they are of a safe size to survive anesthesia.

How Long Will My Persian Live?

An altered Persian can be expected to live to the age of 20, provided regular dental care is given and access to the outside world is restricted. This is not to say that it will not fall victim to a young child opening the doors, your coursing hound, or the neglectful checking of the clothes dryer. Similarly, inherited or infectious diseases may also necessitate an early trip to the veterinarian for euthanasia.

Now that owners are becoming more educated about maintaining veterinary care for aging cats, cat food producers are producing better-quality foods, and veterinarians are being trained for small animal health issues, cats are outliving dogs by almost ten years.

The Final Visit

A major accident, some chronic incurable disease, or simply the infirmities of old age may leave a cat in a state where it will not be able to live again free of pain or able to eat. If this is the case, you should have the animal put to sleep by the veterinarian—euthanasia. It is wise to have a friend accompany you to and from the clinic, or take a taxi home. Take a favorite blanket to give the cat a familiar smell. The staff at the clinic will give your kitty back to you wrapped in this blanket.

If you do feel able to help in this final time, you will want to hold your cat to ease its anxiety and let yours be the final and familiar voice it hears comforting him. This will be the hardest thing you have ever done. Speak quietly the familiar words of love and scratch that secret place under the chin. It may be the hardest and most treasured moment for the two of you. The cat should not experience any further fear or pain, especially if you have the fortitude to hold your pet while the final dose of anesthesia is administered. The dose will be an overdose of the drug used for painless surgery, and your cat will simply close its eyes, and stop breathing. Do not be afraid to break down and cry; there is no shame in the grief of losing a beloved companion. It is likely your veterinarian and his or her assistants will be crying as well; it is easy only on the pet that has passed on.

You can have the cat cremated or disposed of through the veterinarian rendering the service, and there will be a charge for that as well. Arrange this in advance, as likely you will be in no condition to make these decisions on the chosen day. Or you can pick a favorite spot at home, have the space already cleared, and a rosebush ready to put over the grave. A rosebush or other thorny bush planted over the grave will discourage predators or sharp-nosed dogs from disturbing the gravesite.

Grieving

There is no timetable for grief; losing a pet is very much like losing any other member of the family. Expressions of consolation seem at times to be backed by the puzzlement of your friends. It was only a cat; you can get another on any street corner. No, it wasn't.

It was a friend that slept by your bed, or on your pillow, that forced you from bed on those days when you simply wanted the world to go away. Some communities have support groups to help with the loss of your beloved pet.

Filling the Void

One advantage to a pedigreed cat is that it behaves in an expected and predictable way determined by its selected inheritance. This makes it possible to fill that big hole left in your life by the death of your Persian. Do not think of it as a replacement, but as filling that void.

There is really no replacing the completely familiar whims and foibles that come from sharing your life for 20 years with a particular pedigreed Persian. You will be able to find another companion, hopefully from the same breeder of your first, or your third, Persian.

INFORMATION

Useful Books

Fritzsche, Helga. *Cats*. Hauppauge, New York: Barron's Educational Series, Inc., 1982.

Frye, Fredric L., DVM. *First Aid for Your Cat*. Hauppauge, New York: Barron's Educational Series, Inc., 1987.

Müller, Ulrike. *Longhaired Cats*. Hauppauge, New York: Barron's Educational Series, Inc., 1984.

Pond, Grace. *Longhair Cats*. Hauppauge, New York: Barron's Educational Series, Inc., 1984.

Viner, Bradley, DVM. *The Cat Care Manual*. Hauppauge, New York: Barron's Educational Series, Inc., 1986.

Magazines

The Cat Fanciers' Almanac
Cat Fanciers' Association
P.O. Box 1005
Manasquan, NJ 08736-0805
Phone: (732) 528-9797
http://www.cfainc.org/

Cat Fancy Magazine
P.O. Box 2431
Boulder, CO 80321
www.catfancy.com/

Cats Magazine
P.O. Box 83048
Lincoln, NE 68501

CFA Yearbook
Cat Fanciers' Association
P.O. Box 1005
Manasquan, NJ 08736-0805
Phone: (732) 528-9797
http://www.cfainc.org/

Breed Magazines

Cat Tracks (Himalayans)
Atlantic Himalayan Club—Membership
167 West Genesee Street
Chittenango, NY 13037

Persian News
1099 Columbus Avenue, Unit #1
Chico, CA 95926
http://internetofframp.com/persiannews

P and E Cats Online
The only online magazine devoted to Persians
http://www.pandecats.com/

United Silver Fanciers Quarterly
3601 Dovewood Drive
Charlotte, NC 28226-6611
http://www.geocities.com/usfanciers/

Cat Associations

American Cat Association, Inc.,
    the oldest American Association
801 Katherine Avenue
Panorama City, CA 91402
Phone: (818) 781-5656

American Cat Fanciers' Association, Inc.
P.O. Box 1949
Nixa, MO 65714-1949
Phone: (417) 725-1530
http://www.adfacat.com/

Canadian Cat Association
289 Rutherford Road, S, #18
Brampton, Ontario
Canada L6W 3Z9
Phone: (905) 459-1481
http://www.cca-afc.com/

Cat Fanciers' Association, Inc.,
the largest U.S. organization
P.O. Box 1005
Manasquan, NJ 08736-0805
Phone: (732) 528-9797
http://www.cfainc.org/

Cat Fanciers' Federation, Inc.
Ms. Barbara Haley
P.O. Box 661
Gratis, OH 45330
Phone: (937) 787-9009
http://cffinc.org

The "lion cut." Your groomer or veterinarian can shave the body to avoid shedding problems through the spring and summer. Don't shave the tail tip, though! The cat may then treat the tail tip like prey and mutilate it.

The International Cat Association
P.O. Box 2684
Harlingen, TX 78551
Phone: (956) 428-8046
Fax: (956) 428-8047
http://www.tica.org/

Useful Web Sites

Feline Health Issues   *http://cfa.org/caring.html*

Polycystic Kidney Disease   *http://www.indyweb.net/~lucky/Stats.html*

Progressive Retinal Atrophy   *http://www.geocities.com/labonita_persians/felinePRA.html*

Show Schedule for CFA   *http://www.cfa.org/exhibitors/show-schedule.html*

Junior Showmanship   *http://www.cfainc.org/shows/jr-showmanship.html*

Persian Rescue/Adoption   *http://www.felinerescue.net/persianrescuelinks.htm*

I N D E X

About the Authors

Ulrike Müller has bred pedigreed cats for many years, has been a judge at international cat shows, and is the author of several books about cats.

Colleen Power, an emeritus faculty member at California State University at Chico, is editor and publisher of *Persian News*. She has bred pedigreed cats for more than 40 years and has published articles and chapters in various cat books. *Persian Cats* is her first book for Barron's.

Photo Credits

Norvia Behling: 40, 45 (top), 48, 52 (bottom), 53 (top), 57, 68 (center), 69 (top and bottom left), and 89; Richard Chanan: 12 (bottom), 13 (bottom), 16 (top right), 20 (top), 21 (top), 24, 25, 28, 29, 33, 37, 41, 44 (top), 52 (top left and right), 53 (bottom), 56, 64, 68 (top right), 72, 73, 84, and 88; Tara Darling: 16 (bottom left), 21 (bottom), and 32 (top); Isabelle Francais: 2–3, 4, 5, 8, 9, 12 (top), 13 (top), 16 (top left and bottom right), 17 (top and bottom), 20 (bottom), 32 (bottom), 36, 44 (bottom), 45 (bottom), 49, 65, 68 (top left), 85, and 93; and Judith Strom: 68 (bottom), 69 (bottom right).

Important Note

This pet owner's manual tells the reader how to buy or adopt, and care for a Persian cat. The authors and publisher consider it important to point out that the advice given in this book is meant primarily for normally developed cats of excellent physical health and good character.

Anyone who adopts a fully-grown cat should be aware that the animal has already formed its basic impressions of human beings. The new owner should watch the animal carefully, including its behavior toward humans, and should meet the previous owner.

Caution is further advised in the association of children with cats, in meeting with other cats, and in exercising the cat without proper safeguards.

Even well-behaved and carefully supervised cats sometimes do damage to someone else's property or cause accidents. It is therefore in the owner's interest be adequately insured against such eventualities, and we strongly urge all cat owners to purchase a liability policy that covers their cat(s).

Cover Photos

Norvia Behling: back cover; Isabelle Francais: front cover and inside front cover; and Judith Strom: inside back cover.

English translation © copyright 2004, 1990 by Barron's Educational Series, Inc.

Translated from the German by Rita and Robert Kimber.

Originally published in German as *Perserkatzen*.

© copyright 1989 by Gräfe and Unzer GmbH, Munich, Germany.

All rights reserved.
No part of this book may be reproduced in any form, by photostat, microfilm, xerography, or any other means, or incorporated into any information retrieval system, electronic or mechanical, without the written permission of the copyright owner.

All inquiries should be addressed to:
Barron's Educational Series, Inc.
250 Wireless Boulevard
Hauppauge, NY 11788
http://www.barronseduc.com

International Standard Book No. 0-7641-2919-8

Library of Congress Catalog Card No. 2004046182

Library of Congress Cataloging-in-Publication Data
Müller, Ulrike.
  Persian cats : everything about purchase, care, nutrition, disease, and behavior / Ulrike Müller and Colleen Power, with drawings by Fritz W. Köhler.—2nd ed.
    p. cm.
  Includes bibliographical references (p.   ).
  ISBN 0-7641-2919-8 (alk. paper)
    1. Persian cat. I. Vriends, Matthew M. II. Power, Colleen J. III. Title

SF449.P4M85 2004
639.8'32—dc22   2004046182

Printed in China
9 8 7 6 5 4 3 2

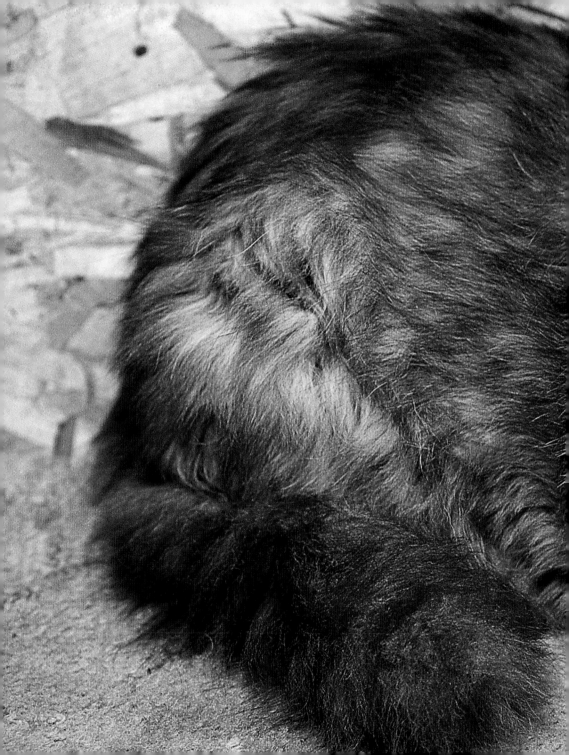